The business world routinely hires by convention and develops leaders by convention. In doing so it makes leaders conform to an accepted box of leadership practices and squashes any real chance of exceptionalism. It places trust in financial systems and automated processes over the individual ability of people.

An Unconventional Leader

offers new and existing leaders an alternative view—a counterpoint that places trust first and foremost in people. A view that challenges the validity and purpose of current workplace conventions. In the process my wish is that this view starts a revolution in how we lead and manage people and, more importantly, in how we all deserve to be managed.

An Unconventional Leader

NEILL WALLACE

ARCHWAY
PUBLISHING

Archway Publishing books may be ordered through booksellers or by contacting:

Archway Publishing
1663 Liberty Drive
Bloomington, IN 47403
www.archwaypublishing.com
1-(888)-242-5904

Cover graphics/art © Michael Sanderson

ISBN: 978-1-4808-1021-1 (e)
ISBN: 978-1-4808-1020-4 (sc)
ISBN: 978-1-4808-1022-8 (hc)

Library of Congress Control Number: 2014914718

Printed in the United States of America

Archway Publishing rev. date: 10/28/2014

MY THANKS

To the many people it was my honor and
privilege to have led and guided.
Thank you for letting me be a part of your journey.

YOUR KIND WORDS

I was a little unsure of what to expect from Neill as a boss
at first, but I knew it probably would be fun. In addition, I
also found it to be both motivational and educational.

In the last two years, Neill has provided me with more direction
and strategic insight than I have received in my entire career.

When I started working with Neill, I was unsure of where
I wanted to go, but over time his belief in me led me to
aspire to increased leadership and responsibility.

EXCEPTIONALISM

The perception that a country, society, institution,
movement, or time period is "exceptional" (i.e., unusual
or extraordinary) in some way and thus does not need
to conform to normal rules or general principles.
Used in this sense, the term reflects a belief formed by lived
experience, ideology, perceptual frames, or perspectives influenced
by knowledge of historical or comparative circumstances.

REVOLUTION

A fundamental change in the way of thinking
about or visualizing something.

Contents

Introduction

This book originated from my experience in trying to determine what I wanted to do with my life. I had just said good-bye to a successful corporate career and high-paying job. It was a career that while financially beneficial had made me feel restrained and left me sapped of my energy, my time, and my faith in corporate America. In leaving I had also said hello to an uncertain yet hopefully unrestrained future. But I wasn't scared and I wasn't worried. Well maybe just a little.

Having taken a few months off to clear my head and renew my spirit, I was pretty sure I did not want to work in the business world anymore. But like a lot of people, when the paychecks stopped coming in, I panicked, just a little. I started to question if the role of the struggling artist was really for me. As a result I started applying for jobs that I believed I was well suited for if not overly excited about. After about a month of sending out resumes, I had heard nothing from any of the companies I had applied to. Thinking I was applying above my qualification level, I changed strategy and applied for jobs I had done years previously. Still nothing. What was going on? I knew it was a competitive market but still.

I sought out advice from friends who were experts in the area of hiring. The feedback from those friends was that my resume was too out of the box and unexpected. Personally I didn't think leading with my passion for transformative leadership and strategic goal setting was a particularly bad thing. Or that focusing on team-led achievements was less desirable than the "I did this" or "I did that" of many resumes I had seen during my career. Only apparently it was.

My friends explained that job recruiters look for key words that demonstrate experience and technical proficiency. "Visionary" and "transformative" were apparently not key words that were going to get any recruiters' attention. Curious, I started applying for jobs that I knew I could do in my sleep. You guessed it, silence.

Now it could be I was really not the great job candidate I thought I was. That really is quite possible. I have a social sciences degree, and my professional experience is mostly limited to banking and medical device companies. Not to mention an apparent rather unusual resume. But it did make me wonder if something else was going on—something that perpetuates the lack of visionary and strong leadership we see today. Was my lack of convention to the normal rules of business to blame, and could they see from my resume that was I likely to defy them? I thought about the unusual path my life had followed. I reflected on my career and on my willingness to break accepted norms. I talked to people to understand their perceptions of contemporary leadership. The result is this book.

An Unconventional Leader is about how we all have the ability to push aside accepted conventions in order to elevate the way we view leadership. I know from my own experiences that it is possible for us all to put aside our ideological thoughts and biases. We can understand, address, and change our motivations and find and understand what inspires us. We can put people first and achieve positive results without having to sacrifice the sometimes excessive numbers game demands of business owners. We can truly listen to, get to know, understand, and inspire our team members, engaging and motivating them along the way. As a result, making a positive change to the culture of your organization.

To achieve a positive personal transformation requires you to challenge commonly accepted, conventional, business leadership behaviors.

It will probably rock the boat and cause you some discomfort. It will take some time and patience. But I am here to help.

An Unconventional Leader literally starts with me, but at its heart and in its purpose, it is actually a journey of transformation that starts with you. It is a call to action for all leaders to be great and for all employees to demand greatness. Unlike many leadership books I have read, it is straightforward and makes no guarantees of success. Like those books though, *An Unconventional Leader* is just one man's view. The view is just seen through a different, alternative lens. It contains anecdotes from my experiences as a leader and as an employee being led. It draws often on a group of men, polar explorers, who have inspired me, and equally as often on the people who gave me the opportunity and encouragement, sometimes grudgingly, to be the leader I was. But this book is not really about them or me at all. It is about us all and the belief that there are different types of leadership we can aspire to and that a "people-first" approach is an acceptable way to ensure long-term sustainable growth *and* a positive business culture.

The goal of *An Unconventional Leader* is to provide existing and potential leaders with an alternative strategy to help them with their career transition and progression. The narrative of the book is drawn from my own practical experience.

I hope this book and specifically the action plan at the end emboldens new leaders to enter a new stage of their career. A stage where they are confident that they know the type of leader they are and are equipped with the knowledge and skills needed to be successful. In the process, you will help make your self and your work environment just a little bit more, well, unconventional.

1. Roads

Conventional wisdom. Two words that are used together often. Indeed you have probably used them yourself. But what exactly is convention and what makes it wise? By definition conventional wisdom is a group of general principles that are commonly accepted as being true. They are accepted as true because experts agree that they are true. They are a staple of everyday life and are what keeps us from walking into a fire or gambling our life savings away on one spin of the roulette wheel. Conventions are like roads that guide us to safety and security. Roads that keep us on the straight and narrow.

Conventions are also especially prevalent in the workplace. Any person who has ever worked anywhere knows that there are generally accepted principles in the workplace around behavior and performance expectations. Not to mention around the amount of time we are supposed to sit at our desks and the endless meetings we are supposed to attend. But what about in leadership? Unsurprisingly, there are plenty of conventions in leadership too. As in life, leadership conventions keep us from walking into the proverbial workplace fire and from throwing our hard-earned salaries away. They also, ironically, prevent many of us from realizing our own unique, natural and, perhaps, exceptional leadership potential.

The very definition of exceptionalism is the lack of conformity to generally accepted principles. In his book, *Endurance: Shackleton's Incredible Voyage*, author Alfred Lansing writes, "the great leaders of historical record have rarely fitted any conventional mold."[1] Yet, in business, fitting leaders into a conventional mold is exactly what we attempt to do. As a result, we are expected to conform to the conventional view of modern corporate leaders: tough, masculine, ego driven, and loyal. We are indoctrinated to believe that in order to succeed we must look and act a certain way. We must follow the conventional rules or face a career that will be going, most likely, nowhere.

To reinforce contemporary leadership characteristics and to ensure we follow the rules, subtle and some not so subtle things happen around us all the time. We are sent on course after course to learn formulaic, rigidly structured principles in an attempt to "teach" us how to be great. We learn some flavor-of-the-month technique, utilize it (perhaps), and then wait until the next leadership fad course comes along. It is a cycle many of us know well. It is frustrating, predictable, and usually pointless. Even more frustrating for potential leaders is the good courses that do teach valuable skills that would allow them to be great (time management, scorecard tracking, etc.), get lost without a needed foundational context (why am I doing this?). Without context they are, for the most part, a waste of time. Some of us may be given a leadership management book, which is intended to inspire us to improve. It is given with little thought of whether or not we find the subject inspiring. It too probably has no foundational context. We will probably assume it is just part of another fad.

Conventional practices also are reinforced by us through imitation. We have seen our boss succeed so we attempt to model ourselves on their behavior and characteristics. Sometimes because we think that is what we should do and sometimes to just flatter their ego. The behavior may seem uncomfortable to us but still we attempt to become

---

[1] Alfred Lansing.

like them. In turn though your boss' behavior was likely born from the conventional behavior they had seen in their leaders. It is another cycle that keeps the rules of conventional career behavior in check.

As employees and potential leaders we eventually become bewildered, bemused, and demotivated. The thought of another course to attend or book to read induces nausea. Imitation becomes emotionally draining. We lose the will to argue against the banality of it all. Who can really blame us for opting to stick with convention?

If there was a conventional wisdom dictionary, it probably would define leadership by using three key tasks: financial, strategic, and people management. Experts would agree that leaders need to be financially responsible and strategic in nature. They also must have the ability to carefully manage their teams. The key tasks seem simple in words if not necessarily in execution. To help us execute the three tasks, there is a distinctly marked management highway all leaders are expected to follow. Signposts planted by our executive bosses tell us where we should be strategically headed and financially focused. Road markings painted by human resources personnel and external education partners define the parameters for training and coaching our teams. A comfortable tarmac, paved by indoctrinated behavioral practices, keeps us from veering too far off the road.

The conventional leadership road works great in principle and sometimes in practice, especially when the climate is good for traveling. But what happens when the signs are not clear or you receive conflicting directions? What should you do when the parameters for training are uncomfortable and simply have no context to help you make any sense of them? What happens when convention fails us? The answer, it seems, is not much happens. At least nothing that furthers the quest for good leadership.

Today many of us just accept that the leadership pathway is not only unchallengeable but also unchangeable. Take, for example, leadership in the United States Congress. The prevailing opinion, or conventional wisdom, in the United States around the people making the laws and decisions that impact our lives, is that there is a crisis in leadership. Opinion polls show approval ratings for Congress at all-time lows. Single digits. Gasp. But why? Politicians are divided along figurative and literal ideological aisles and rarely do we see them working together productively for the greater good. We know that their pandering actions to a core electoral base are inspired by a need to stay in power and not to be great.

Political conventional wisdom applauds and rewards length of service over quality of service. As a result the motivation is to stay in power, not actually do some good. Getting elected and staying elected is the goal. Motivated by winning reelection (politics, like business, is after all a numbers game), politicians pander to the folks who help them achieve that goal. By pandering they make us feel like we, as citizens and voters, play second fiddle to big money corporate and wealthy individual donors. We know when they speak that they are not really talking to us.

Yet those same opinion polls show that when it comes to our own congressional representatives, we actually quite like them and often reelect them, over and over. Conventional wisdom seems to be that my representative is bad, but not as bad as your representative somewhere else. (Incidentally this belief is consistent with the convention that says it also must be somebody else's fault.) There is also the prevailing belief is that there is very little we can really do about it. That we really only have two options. We either take up the fight and rebel, as many people who have felt oppressed have done. Or we just do nothing, accepting things are just the way they are. Accept the convention.

It is not too much of a stretch to believe the state of leadership in Washington is not just an isolated political one, but rather that it is a leadership dearth in general. Think about corporate America and the state of leadership in offices across the nation. Does your boss seem to be driven by some rigid, unequivocal ideological ideal? Do they seem motivated by a need to pander to their boss and not rock the boat so they can stay in their leadership role? Do you believe you are playing second fiddle in their actions to the demands of owners and stake-holders? Are they really listening to you? Are they holding themselves accountable, or are mistakes someone else's fault, like yours? I would not be surprised if you are nodding yes to at least some of these ques-tions. But you also might be thinking that at least your boss is not as bad as someone elses. Better the devil you know and all that. As a result you decide to not rock the boat and informally "reelect" your boss by choosing to accept conventional wisdom and carry on doing your job the way you are expected to do it. No need to get burned or gamble on a spin of the wheel unless you need to, right? After all, it's not your fault they are how they are. Rebellion against convention just doesn't seem like a good option. Or is it?

I, like many of us, have always admired the rebels, the ground-breakers, the unconventional. They are after all the people who actu-ally make change happen. Two men who have inspired me, through-out out my life and professional career, to veer off the convention-paved pathway, to rebel, are the men of polar exploration, Roald Amundsen and Ernest Shackleton. I know they are hardly household names. You don't see the face of Shackleton on too many t-shirts worn by angst-ridden teens. Yet they have provided me with many teachable moments throughout my life and career. They gave me the inspiration to see the world and the workplace differently. They changed my view of what it means to be a leader. They were both, in their own ways, rebels with a strategic cause.

Roald Amundsen was born in Borge, Norway, on July 16, 1872, while that nation was still under the rule of neighboring Sweden. As a teenager he had been inspired by countryman Fridjtof Nansen's successful crossing of Greenland in 1888.[2] The crossing was an in-ternational event that brought pride to the Norwegian people. As

---

[2] Roland Huntford.

a result, the young Amundsen dreamed of adventures on the sea and bringing further pride to his country. But Amundsen's mother wanted him to be a doctor, so the obedient son went to university to study medicine in order to please her. (Pleasing our mothers is clearly a convention that transcends all generations and nationalities). When she passed away though, he was free of that convention and quit his studies for a life on the seas. In 1903, Amundsen led the first expedition to cross the Northwest Passage. On his return to Norway, he became a sensation and a national hero. It is well documented that he had a hunger for knowledge and took in any piece of information he thought could later help him. Much of the knowledge he gained during the Northwest Passage voyage he took with him to the South Pole. On December 14, 1911, Amundsen and his team became the first people to reach the South Pole, more than a month before the rival British-led Robert Scott exploration team arrived at the same spot.

Ernest Shackleton also had a Robert Scott connection. He traveled along with Scott on the 1901-04 *Discovery* expedition. That trip sowed the seeds of his deep-rooted scorn of Scott.[3] It also probably reinforced his disdain for conventional norms, which Scott epitomized. Born in Ireland in 1874, Shackleton's family moved to England when he was ten. It is said that he had a sense of adventure even as a child. Despite being characterized during his merchant navy career as a loner, Shackleton was renowned by his fellow team members as being an effective communicator who could keep a mood light, even in the direst of situations. In 1907 he returned to the Antarctic to lead a team to reach the South Pole. Worried about insufficient food supplies for the return journey, Shackleton turned the team around just 112 miles short of their goal and, in doing so, saved his life and the lives of his team. During the return journey, and in an act of great sacrifice, Shackleton gave up his one allotted daily biscuit to Jack Wild. Wild would later write in his diary that

---

[3] Roland Huntford.

it was an act of great sacrifice that would never leave his memory.[4] The adventure that Shackleton is most well known for, however, is the ill-fated, yet miraculous trip of the aptly titled *Endurance* in 1914. Books have been written and films made about his legendary leadership in defying unbelievable odds to keep his team alive. Shackleton has also been used in leadership books and courses as an example of how a people-centered approach can be a tool for any modern-day leader.[5] His leadership style defied the time in which he lived. He was a determined, calculating risk-taker, and most of all, unconventional. He is buried on the island of South Georgia in the South Atlantic Ocean, his spiritual home for many reasons familiar to any Shackleton devotee. Ernest Shackleton remains today the historical figure I admire above all others and the one who I aspire to be the most like. He has been my greatest leadership teacher.

While Amundsen and Shackleton have taught me about great adventure and leadership, Robert Falcon Scott offered me an alternative, seemingly more conventional, view of team management. Indeed I have always interpreted his story as more of a cautionary tale against being too conventional, especially in an unconventional climate like the Antarctic, or business. Born in 1868 in Devon, England, Scott took the traditional career pathway for any aspiring, career-driven Victorian Englishman and joined the navy.[6] With the death of his father, a looming family financial crisis, and then the death of his brother Archie, Scott felt an enormous burden to succeed in his naval career. As a result he sought opportunities to make himself stand out among his peers.[7] Such an opportunity presented itself when he met Charles Markham, then president of the Royal Geographical Society (RGS). Scott learned of a planned Antarctic expedition, *Discovery*, and volunteered to lead it despite never having shown the slightest interest

---

4 Leif Mills.
5 Stephanie Barczewski.
6 David Crane.
7 Ranulph Fiennes.

in polar exploration. The association with the RGS ensured that all of Scott's expeditions to the Antarctic would have a scientific as well as exploratory purpose. His attempt to reach the South Pole was his third trip to Antarctica. In contrast to Amundsen's attempt, with its conservative estimations of anticipated climate and food needs, among others, Scott's planning contained no margin of error. Food needs deposited in stores for the return journey from the pole were calculated assuming everything would go off perfectly. As is often the case with any strategic adventure, it didn't. It would result in Scott and the members of his South Pole team paying the ultimate price.

The comparisons between Scott and contemporary leadership are both metaphorical and literal. For the time, Scott's chosen career path and leadership style were very conventional, and parallels can still be drawn today. He chose a career route through the military that would most likely lead to the career advancement and subsequent financial success he desired. Today we learn that we need to go to college and gain a degree in our specific chosen field to obtain promotions. Scott led his polar team with a reliance on traditional hierarchical ideas, as well as tried and trusted, if not always appropriate, equipment and approaches. Modern leadership organizational charts are still extremely vertical and many training techniques still cater to a financial numbers first approach. Scott feigned unconventional paths, even using the same route to the pole that Shackleton had used in 1907, a literal already traveled path.

As Scott is to convention and the well-traveled path, Amundsen and Shackleton were, excuse the pun, the quintessential polar opposites. Amundsen liked to absorb information from new ideas and different cultures to push the polar exploration envelope. He was a fastidious planner who would check and double-check. He would fine-tune plans up until the last moment. He had time to seek out information because he scheduled most of his time to doing just that. He scheduled time to learn, to understand, to plan. He was able to schedule time because he was well organized and saw obtaining information as a necessary task. It was, in fact, the most important task to him. Amundsen also showed no fear of uncharted paths as evidenced by his successful crossing of the Northwest Passage and his novel route to the South Pole. He judged talent and skill on demonstrated ability and not on status or ranking. He felt a duty to his team, long after the explorations were over.

Shackleton similarly felt an enormous duty as a leader for his team's safety, and the well-being of his team trumped any personal success or achievement. He led when strong decisions were needed but also intuitively knew when to place trust and responsibility in his team. Shackleton made a career of defying conventional rules of, well, a career, and success for him was defined by the journey, not the destination. Like Amundsen, he led with a people-first attitude, and in doing so they both charted a new approach to leadership via a less traveled, unconventional road.

Many of us willingly accept that there is just the one leadership road we can take. Convention and fear keep us from attempting a different route. But great leaders like Amundsen and Shackleton have taken the unconventional road and been successful. They have been willing to put their personal achievements aside in order for their teams to succeed. Rather than leading with a culture of fear, they promoted an altruistic people-first attitude.

I am familiar with the people-first approach. I spent many years at a company that promoted, with good reason, that people were its greatest asset. It was an ethos that attracted me and many others to the company. It was a company whose growth was also significantly higher than industry averages. It was an exciting place to work, and I took pride in being associated with a company that truly lived a people-focused mission. It was like being on my own little polar exploration. A few years into my career, the company underwent a department-wide process improvement drive to refine efficiencies and financial performance. Scorecards were brought in, charts and displays decorated the hallways, and presentations were made regularly on department savings. It seemed at the time like a positive move and I firmly believed in the program. The people-first approach and financial efficiency model worked together well, allowing the company to be cavalier and dynamic but not reckless and inefficient. Additionally employees felt like they were directly contributing to the company's success, which in turn helped to promote the positive culture that existed and the people-first values of the organization. It wasn't the South Pole but it was still exciting.

Then a change in the parent company's top management occurred. Around the same time the external environment also started to change. The company's industry market size stagnated and customers starting rejecting innovative but costly products in favor of mass availability and lower pricing. The changes to the external environment were making the company's high revenue growth numbers of the past years more difficult. In reaction to the external environment, the focus at the company shifted—at first awkwardly and then sharply—from a people-first/process-improvement numbers game to just a plain old numbers game. The company swiftly moved from being people centric to not even playing the people game at all.

Slowly, in unison, the company culture changed and morale started to decline. Creative output seemed to slow. The company succumbed to the convention that says when times start getting tough, you start acting tough. Tough on budgets, tough on expenses, and tough on your people. It is a business management story as old as time and quite predictable. Balance sheet numbers first, trust in people second. I don't know all the answers as to why the change occurred where I worked, and there are probably hundreds of them, but succumbing to conventional norm appeared to be one of them. Rather than remaining brazen and pioneering with a differing approach that diverged from the normal business pathway, when times got difficult, the company sped fast to meet up with the conventional road. As a consequence, the core belief in people and the values that come with that, were seemingly sacrificed.

The changes at my former company are a story that many of you may know well. During the recent global economic crisis employees had their benefits reduced or taken away, hours cut back, and many millions lost their jobs. Work demands increased along with the fear of losing our livelihoods. Leaders were applauded and rewarded for making the drastic changes to keep profits looking good. To the unconventional mind though they took the easy road. A road that reduced people to mere cogs in a process. People were left on the ice flows of uncertainty not perhaps because leaders wanted to leave them, but because it was the conventional response to do so.

Good and bad leaders follow the conventional path, but the great, inspiring leaders don't need it. Nelson Mandela defied convention by choosing to work with the people who had held him captive rather than take the anticipated revenge on them. He took the proverbial high road. Mary Kay Ash, founder and CEO of Mary Kay Cosmetics, challenged and proved wrong the prevailing conventional rule of the time that only men could create, lead, and manage a successful business. She built a brand new road for many women to follow down. Bill Gates defied the required college degree convention and helped create a technology revolution. He took a road that we are told is too dangerous to travel down.

The roads all of these great leaders traveled, including Amundsen and Shackleton, were neither guided nor smooth nor easy. Yet they all succeeded at being inspiring, successful leaders. They are all in their own unique ways exceptional. They are unconventional leaders.

If, as a leader, you believe that people are your greatest asset and you have a culture of people-led process improvement, it would seem obvious that a process-improvement project to adjust a business climate-change tide would involve the people who can influence the company's culture and morale the most; its leaders. The desired result with this book is, in essence, a process improvement in leadership. A process improvement that demonstrates there is an alternative leadership road to travel. That there can be a change in thinking that emboldens leaders to trust in a people-first approach through both the good and the not-so-good times. It is an improvement that can lead to stable businesses that benefit all stakeholders without the sacrifice of core values and beliefs. Ultimately, it is an improvement that can lead to more inspiring and successful leadership with more fully realized leaders.

Throughout the rest of this book I will look at leadership conventions and challenge them. I will explore (sorry, another bad pun) and challenge conventions around time management, hiring, job descriptions, honesty, people development, and goal setting, to name a few. I believe that until we all, or at least most of us, begin to challenge conventional wisdom around what is means to act and behave like a leader, we will never achieve the type of revolutionary change needed to alter the current view of leadership.

We must always remember with gratitude and admiration the first sailors who steered their vessels through storms and mists, and increased our knowledge of the lands of ice in the South.

—ROALD AMUNDSEN

2. A Fish out of Water

I never really fitted the mold of the typical business executive. I was not part of some good old boys' network or management fraternity group. I endured, though occasionally enjoyed, socializing and drinking with other executives as part of my job, but most of the time gleaned no real lasting satisfaction from it. I didn't have pictures of a wife or children scattered about my desk. I talked loudly, often, and without an appropriate business talk filter equally as often. Don't get me wrong, I could hang with other execs when needed, discussing sports and telling jokes. But I hated playing corporate politics and always saw myself as an individual first, a regular employee second, and an executive last. When it came to leadership, I just as equally felt like a fish out of water. I never seemed to quite understand that in the business world, straying from conventional leadership norms was practically forbidden behavior. It was a taboo I broke often. Yet marching to the beat of my own drum is exactly what set me apart from the conventional norm and allowed me to succeed.

In 2004 I was given an opportunity that I was only afforded because a great leader, an unconventional leader, saw something in me. On paper I was probably not a stand-out candidate for the role of helping to grow the international business at a medical device company.

(I had little sales management experience and absolutely no medical device industry experience.) By applying what I had learned (and was constantly relearning), adopting a people-first approach, and having the support, if not total understanding, of some great and well-intentioned bosses, in the space of nine years I was promoted progressively from a business development associate, to sales operations manager, to director of international business, and finally to senior director of global sales and marketing. And, for most of the time, I did it my way. A way that emphasized putting people first and valued the power of transformative and inspiring leadership. A way that often defied normal conventions.

Now, with the mere mention of the words "people" and "first," some of you already may be thinking to yourself that I was the sort of leader who thinks smiles and hugs make profits and balance sheets look good. "Soft" is the word that probably springs to mind. If believing in a people-first approach makes a person soft, then I am guilty, and you may be right in your assessment of me. But that would be simplifying the approach I took and the emphasis of this book. It would also mean assuming that a people-first approach can't also reap financial benefits to an organization, which it can. I am proof of that, and there are many books and articles written about the positive economic outcomes for organizations that adhere to the people-first approach.

The assumption of "softness" also would be overlooking that during my career I have made difficult decisions. I demoted and fired people, though only after thorough personnel developmental plans failed to work. I fully implemented and managed strategic management systems to track short and long-term goals, with the full participation of teams. I helped develop processes to ensure that unprofitable business segments became profitable and oversaw departmental expenditures to a cost-control target (that incidentally were often more stringent than those of my peers who may have accused me of being soft). I embraced the philosophy of process improvement long before it was fashionable and required a financial number to back it up. I reprimanded people in the external environment for unacceptable attitudes and behavior. I was tough in defense of my team members when they were right and had enough fortitude to admit errors when we were wrong.

If believing in the concept of putting people first and knowing the value of a highly engaged, skilled, and committed team makes me soft, then I am proudly soft. In reply I would tell you that putting people first is an attitude, not an expense on a profit and loss statement. I would tell you that as a leadership tool it works just as effectively as a culture of fear and numbers. That not trusting in yourself and your team is just an attitude. An attitude that is sadly all too, well, unconventional.

Today many employees bemoan a lack of leadership and the "must be busy-busy" work culture. Yet it is the organization itself that creates the type of climate that eventually leads to the leadership dearth. Conventional recruiting practices that focus on hiring technical ability and education, combined with a task-focused culture set the tone. They are hiring practices that would never have given rebels like myself an opportunity. And it is a task-centric culture that doesn't allow people the time to truly lead or to develop into a leader.

Leadership is like air for businesses. They need it to function, pay little attention to it until it starts to disappear, and die without it. Little value though is placed on leadership as a skill, despite the fact that businesses need it just to survive, let alone thrive. This is especially true when it comes to recruiting company positions. As a result of not hiring at least some potential leaders, companies slowly start starving themselves of corporate air. Over time, the existing vision and team-focused leaders start to leave and are replaced by technically competent individuals. The company air gets thinner, and it becomes harder for everyone at the organization to breathe. Unless an intervention occurs, a slow, painful death is inevitable. We know that good leaders have transformative skills that create vision and growth for an organization. They also generate engagement and excitement for employees and stakeholders. So why then do companies seemingly not value or recruit the personnel with transformative skills and then not give them the time to lead?

Business is by nature a metric-driven beast. If you can't measure it, it cannot exist. If it can't be quantified, it cannot be of value. It might be hard for leaders to hear, but leadership is rarely considered a measurable or quantifiable skill. In the minds of conventional recruiters, quantifiable success is predicted from candidates who have a solid educational and technical-focused background. Candidates who have true leadership ability but little technical experience will almost certainly be discounted during the resume screening process because of the perception that they won't add any real quantifiable value. The leaders among the applicants won't make it to the interview stage where, in an ironic twist, the inevitable manager-type questions (how would you deal with a subordinate employee blah blah) will be asked.

If rather than assessing leadership ability from a bland and predictable resume form, they instead asked just one or two simple personality style questions, then they may just find that badly needed air. One application question I heard recently asked candidates if they were a crayon, what color crayon would they be. That's it. That was the only question on the application form. The question requires candidates to think. It would demonstrate if the candidate has an understanding who they are and more importantly why. It would be unconventional but it would also make for an interesting and fascinating screening process.

The paradox of conventional hiring to perceived technical ability is that most good leaders will rarely spend their days doing actual technical work. They should be too busy to worry about performing (insert any technical skill here) because they are working too hard to ensure their teams have the ability to perform (insert any technical skill here). They should be spending their days leading and providing the air that keeps the business functioning and moving forward. They should be helping to maintain the corporate culture and reach across departmental lines to ensure consistency and fairness. Leaders take the time to challenge their teams to achieve results beyond what they may have thought possible. They clear hurdles and keep the conduits of communication open and honest. Leaders need to be transparent and direct. A leader stuck in technical minutia cannot possibly have the time to focus on their people. As a result, they are not a leader. Well not a good leader anyway.

How we spend our time as leaders is a well-indoctrinated convention. We are supposed to be networking with other executives, going on power lunches, and generally appearing to be important and busy. Swimming with the other big fish as it were. We are conditioned to become self-important, to believe that we already know the answers. It is people-focused, just the wrong people and the wrong focus. Plus how much new information can you actually gain from this small fish bowl of likeminded thoughts. My time though was spent elsewhere. The information I needed to be a leader was in another bowl.

Like Amundsen, I would try to devote most of my working time to seeking information. To achieve this I would block out large chunks of my calendar for "tasks" and "catch-up." But really it was nothing time. It was time I would spend getting to know, understand, and learn from my team, seeking out new information about the business environment. Like Shackleton I needed time to be available to "rescue" my team members. Okay, not rescue from a capsized ship on a moving ice shelf, but rescue nonetheless. When they needed help or advice, I wanted to be available. When they needed to vent, I wanted to be the person they let their frustrations out on. When they needed a pathway cleared, I wanted to be there to clear that pathway. Convention would say we should be busy, busy, busy. Certainly way too busy to schedule nothing time. And I was busy. But, unconventionally, I was busy spending time with my team. Not "meeting" busy. Not "executive" busy. My main task was to be a leader, and I took that task seriously.

To employees, the emotional consequence of poor leadership is self-evident. To the company, the financial consequences of not recruiting leaders are just as obvious, especially in the long term. In the short term, there is the cost of turning a technically capable employee into a leader. Companies will spend huge amounts of money to send employees in leadership roles to course after course in an attempt to make them leaders. The results in my experience are mixed at best and have little long-term significance. It's not that the courses don't have any educational value, at least in the short term. There are some really good leadership courses, and I have attended many of them. I reference some of them later in this book. It's just that I believe the conventional premise that leadership as a skill can be taught in two and half days in a hotel conference room is incorrect. Leadership, as Mr. Lansing pointed out, is not convention.

Take for example the conventional practice by many hirers of promoting to leadership roles employees who are technically very good at their current job but have exhibited little leadership ability. We do this because technical skill trumps everything, sometimes even attitude, apparently with the assumption that leadership will just happen. It is this convention though that results in great athletes rarely turning out to be great coaches, and why technically skilled employees struggle when they are promoted to leadership positions. Yet technical skill and experience are qualities valued disproportionately over leadership potential and ability by many recruiters. It would seemingly make more short-term financial sense to hire leadership-focused candidates and spend the money getting them the technical knowledge (assuming that is even needed!). I am pretty sure most people would agree it is easier to teach a person technical skills than it is to teach them leadership.

Maybe recruiters just don't understand that leadership is ultimately a quantifiable skill. It can be gauged in the numbers of new ideas created and strategic goals undertaken. It is tangible in the atmosphere of corporate facilities. It can be seen in the faces of the employees and in their attitude to work. It can be measured in results that keep the company adapting to the prevailing climate. When there is leadership air in an organization, there is life. Leadership should be measured in the quality of life of all those involved in the company's performance not just the quality of the financial books. As a result recruiters should, and need to, be able to find and hire those candidates who can and want to breathe life into an organization. Not just know everything about (insert technical skill here). They should want to hire the fish that wants to jump out of the bowl.

We as human beings are complex characters with many innate qualities. Our different genetic makeup and our divergent journeys mean we are driven by different things, see the world in unique ways, and have actions that are neither predictive nor consistent. Some fish, like Amundsen, like Shackleton, like me, are just born to want to jump out of the bowl in which we are placed. We see leadership as the means to the end, the main focus. It does not mean that on everything we are wrong or right. It just means we are different. Different people from the conventional norm who act in ways different from some predetermined, expected behavior. Success for some may come from staying in the bowl. But you have a choice, and it is okay to jump out of the conventional bowl, I promise.

3. Attitude and Nature

I have been a very lucky person. In many ways there have been times when I thought I was charmed. Sadly I am merely human. I have no superpower or lucky leprechaun sprinkling magic dust everywhere I go. If only, right? Opportunities though have fallen into my lap, and even at the worst of times, things always seem to have worked out for me.

One of those not-so-good times was almost immediately after graduating from college in 2001. For a year I tried to find work but was unsuccessful. Not being a permanent resident of the United States at that time, companies were unwilling to go through the cumbersome work-visa process on my behalf, and to be honest, I could hardly blame them. As a result, even if they liked me they would not hire me. During that year I also had a long-term relationship end. For perhaps the first time in my life I was not sure what I was doing, where I was going, or even who I was. After a brief return to my birth country, Australia, I had one of those life-changing events that snaps you back to your senses.

I was sitting on a sofa (which was also my bed) in a friend's living room, my clothes in a suitcase, the remnants of my life in boxes in his garage, hair a mess ... well, you get the idea. Out of nowhere and without really thinking about it, I remembered something my grandmother had once told me: "Breathe in, breathe out, be grateful." I breathed in. I breathed out. I repeated. Gradually, after numerous repetitions, I found some gratitude. Bit by bit I also found some perspective. In a few days I had found my survival instinct again, as simple as that. I got my crap together. When life gives you lemons and all that.

With my senses in order, I started to remember who I was and what I was about. I was still not sure what I was going to do or where I was going professionally, but the core of who I was as a person—a fighter, a survivor, an ideas guy, a rationalist—all came back, and came back strong. Feeling like myself again, things started to fall back into place. Major life crisis averted and major life lesson learned: never forget who you are. More importantly I learned that who you are has needs that must be met. If those needs are not being met, your emotional health suffers tremendously. I needed a creative outlet and security. Neither of those needs were being met sitting on my friends sofa in a self-pity party funk. But when I drew on my personal understanding of who I was, I used it to my advantage to make plans for the next part of my life.

Just as we all share the ability to learn technical skills, we also all have the capability to self-examine. The foundation of being an unconventional leader can only stay strong if you have first undertaken a self-examination. A self-examination that leads to the awareness of what type of leader you are and, perhaps more importantly, what type of leader you want to be. Knowing who you are, what inspires and motivates you, provides the platform for successful, transformative leadership, puts skills training into a valuable context, and allows you to shine without having to compromise who you are.

Acting and being who you are is your greatest strength. Your traits—quirky and odd as some may be, especially to others—are part of your DNA and to fight them is to fight nature itself. To fight nature is exhausting and maybe impossible. That is why the lucky leprechaun magic dust in our lives is merely the depth to which we know ourselves and act accordingly. Why in the workplace we pretend to be something we are not is a mystery to me, and probably to nature herself.

If you want to be an unconventional, people-first-focused leader, your journey has started with believing you have a choice about your leadership style and knowing there are alternative pathways to take toward success. The next step of the journey is knowing what type of leader you are naturally inclined to be. Knowing your natural leadership style can be achieved by doing two things. First, by undertaking an honest assessment of what motivates and inspires you to even be a leader, your leadership attitude. And secondly, by knowing and understanding your natural work style.

The good news for us all is that leadership, at least on paper, really just requires two attributes: technical knowledge and a good attitude. If you are already in a leadership role, there is a high likelihood that you already have the technical part down. Plus you have a team comprised of people with technical expertise. Technical ability and experience are, after all, how we hire. So that just leaves attitude. Attitudes are impacted by our life experiences. For example, if you enjoy the experience of reading this book, you probably will have a positive attitude toward me. What affects our attitudes as leaders are life experiences, which drive our motivations and inspirations.

It is easy to confuse and interchange motivation and inspiration. A simple Google search will glean many definitions of the two words. For me, motivation is doing something for some external, tangible reason (please your manager and get a promotion, receive a "world's best boss" mug from your staff). Inspiration is the soulful, poetic, intangible soundtrack to whatever you are doing.

I am motivated to write this book as a means of getting my unconventional leadership methods out to a broader audience, as well as filling my cathartic need to write. My inspirations are the polar explorers, who have influenced my leadership style, and my friends, who have placed so much trust in my ability to actually write a book. Not to mention a certain basset hound that I will get to later.

Simply put, motivation is internal; inspiration is external. Because of their internal nature, it is easy to misunderstand a person's motivations. No matter how altruistic or unselfish a person's motives, some people will still see them as self-serving. It probably won't matter to some people, even if you told them straight to their face, that you are not particularly motivated by promotion or money or power (or even food and shelter). They might still think you are. But you may be inspired by them to make them change their mind. Consequently, inspiration can affect our actions as much as motivation.

The first step then in understanding your leadership attitude is to ask yourself what motivates you to even want to be a great leader. Motivation is very important here because if you took a leadership position, or want to be leader, in order to buy a fancy new car, you might have taken the position for a good reason, but it is a mediocre reason at best if you want to be a great leader. Perhaps you are okay with mediocrity. Trust me, I have known plenty of leaders who are role models for mediocrity, and they have been successful. But did they do anything great? Did they inspire anyone? Did they make a lasting impression? Probably not. And do you really think their team was happy having a mediocre leader? Leaders who exhibit and practice great leadership, born from a natural motivation, do inspire us and do make a lasting impression. I only had to look to the polar explorers to see the importance of motivation in leadership style.

Amundsen was motivated by a sense of national pride and wanted a global achievement for Norway, his newly independent homeland. He was also motivated by new ideas and thoughts and wanted to learn, learn, and learn. He observed everything, read everything, and listened until he felt he had heard every piece of relevant information possible. Shackleton's motives were also for the grand adventure, a place in history, to be free of the rules of societal conformity that prevailed in Victorian England. It was a time and a place into which he simply could not conform.

Scott was the quintessential career-driven gentlemen to whom financial success, social standing, and name mattered. He believed this could only be achieved through career advancement (perhaps to his detriment), and he viewed the South Pole as a stepping-stone to achieving that goal. Scott, more than Amundsen or Shackleton, wanted the proverbial new car. In going to the Antarctic, Scott defied nature. He had spent time in Antarctica during the *Discovery* expedition of 1901-04, yet he had seemingly learned nothing about how to deal with frigid weather or how to most efficiently traverse hundreds of miles of ice and snow. There was little on his resume or in his leadership style to suggest he could successfully lead a team to the South Pole and back. It turned out he could not.

But in one of life's ironic historical twists, he did achieve the sort of fame—born of an English need at the time for a hero to worship—that arguably Shackleton, and perhaps Amundsen, did crave. Whether that hero worship would have occurred had he survived the South Pole, we will never know. But it is fascinating to conjecture, had he survived, whether or not he would have been truly happy with merely gaining idol status. I suspect he still would have wanted that car.

The polar explorers' motivations helped drive how they defined success. How you choose to define success is a critical element of who you are as a leader and whether or not you will demonstrate great leadership. If you see success as a personal, individual achievement or a stepping-stone toward career advancement, you might be a leader, but you probably won't be exhibiting leadership. You probably won't have the trust or respect of your team either.

Amundsen saw the success of his team being the first men to reach the South Pole as a group effort. He even gave the honor of planting the Norwegian flag into the polar ice to a team member, a powerful and deeply meaningful gesture that demonstrates clearly that Amundsen saw the team's achievement as a group effort. Amundsen's gesture was also profoundly inspiring, at least to me. That is the good thing about inspiration. It is almost omnipresent in life. We can find it in the places we visit, in the actions we see people do, or in events that seem mundane to some but leave a lasting impression on others. You just need to be aware of it and open to it.

Now is the time to share my story of the basset hound. A few years ago I attended a dog agility trial. If you have never seen a dog agility trial, it is where owners or trainers guide their dogs through an obstacle course of teeter-totters, tubes, and poles. The dog that completes the course in the fastest time wins. It is serious stuff for the owners and a big business. The dogs compete in two timed races, one in the morning and the other in the afternoon.

During the break in runs at this particular dog trial, the event held an "open field" test. Any dog could be entered in this test, regardless of skill level, breeding, or lack of either. It was a one-off event where the dog needed to complete the course in a predetermined amount of time in order to pass. Now, because this was an open field, some of the dogs were not very experienced, some not very fast, and some not very comfortable with the various obstacles put in front of them. One dog in particular was all three.

He was this rather largish basset hound with a predisposition to howling, a lot. As the dog's owner brought him up to the start line, it did not seem likely that he would complete the course, let alone do it in the allocated amount of time. And so it was. At the start the dog ambled toward the first hurdle, a literal one-foot-high hurdle, and stopped. The owner screamed words of encouragement at the dog but to no avail. The dog remained firmly entrenched at the base of the hurdle, howling. The owner refused to give up though and continued to clap and yell, egging on the idle dog. Meanwhile the clock let the owner and the crowd know how much time was left, and it was ticking down. Down to one minute. Down to thirty seconds. Down to ten seconds.

The crowd was now engrossed, clapping, cheering, and counting down the seconds. Ten, nine, eight, seven, six, five, four. And then it happened. The dog, with all his effort, jumped over the first hurdle. The owner screamed in delight and ran toward the happiest basset hound you ever saw in your life. The crowd applauded and yelled in approval as if the dog had just won Westminster. It was an exhilarating moment, an inspirational moment. The owner knew the dog would probably never make it through the course. The crowd thought it likely he would not make it over the first hurdle. The dog had probably doubted himself also. But he did it.

It was a minor achievement at a small local event with little or no consequence to the vast majority of people in attendance, let alone the human race, past or present. Yet to me it was poetic, metaphoric, and exhilarating, all at the same time. It was inspiring to me because of the simplicity of the achievement. It was simply a dog and his owner redefining the conventional definitions of success, in a very unconventional way. It was proof to me that not all goals have to be large or audacious and that glory can be defined by the small steps as much as the large ones. I like to believe that at the moment of jumping the hurdle, that basset hound was motivated by the encouragement of his owner and inspired by a desire to please her. It was the "dog-first" attitude that enabled him to overcome whatever shortcomings he might have had about jumping. It was one of the most inspiring things I have ever witnessed and a moment I will never forget.

Your attitude though is just part of knowing who you are as a leader. The other part is knowing your leadership style. Getting to know yourself and spending time understanding your actions and decisions are luxuries rarely afforded us, especially in the business world. I was fortunate to work at a company with a progressive, forward-thinking human resources department.

A few years into my tenure, the human resources department implemented a training program for leaders called MIRRORS. To be honest I could not tell you what the acronym stood for, but it was a pretty clever one because it is so obvious what it represented: look at how you see yourself before you attempt to influence someone else. Genius. For those of you out there without a MIRRORS program, the good news is that there are many reputable courses designed for business professionals that do essentially the same thing, including getting to know yourself.

About ten years ago I took the Taylor Protocols Core Value Index assessment test. It was a breakthrough moment for me in understanding why I had a need to be unconventional. As I said, there are some really good tests that probably could provide equally insightful results. Being unconventional means you should not just take a test because I happened to and found it to be eye opening and career changing. But as my experience was with the Core Values Index (CVI), that is what I will use for this book.

The CVI is a personal trait assessment, with the results calculated by responses to a series of questions. Taylor Protocols describes the assessment like this:

> A revolutionary human assessment that provides a
> description of the innate, unchanging nature of an
> individual, which is different from personality and

behavioral based assessments. This unique instru-
ment takes ten minutes or less to complete, and provides a highly accurate and reliable picture of the core
motivational drivers of any person, with an instant
report, online.

Because it is neither personality nor behavioral based, but rather
deals with the innateness of an individual, the CVI gets to the core
of why we do the things we do. According to my CVI results, my
thinking style is almost equally balanced between being an "innovator" (setting and developing new strategic goals and plans with
well-developed ideas) and the more conservative "banker" (gathering
information, thinking through risk, and maintaining metrics that
measure success or failure).

It is a true, accurate reflection of me. I tend to observe a situation,
taking in information along the way before analyzing it in order to
make a decision. I play devil's advocate, a lot, to ensure all aspects of
a strategic move or business goal are established. I dislike, and have
little time for, people who say something without any basis in fact or
information. I love to brainstorm new ideas and develop strategies,
but equally enjoy spending time balancing the pros and cons of every
possible move. It is little surprise then that my heroes are polar explorers, whose very exploits exemplify the need for a pioneering spirit and
calculated planning.

What I understood, more importantly than understanding my
hero worship, was that the "banker/innovator" diagnosis was not
just an accurate description of my work habits; it was a fair description of how I act and behave in my personal life. When I was in my
early teens, I attended a performing arts school. It was a great way
for me to spend some of my adolescence because it allowed me to
fully embrace my creative, innovative side. At the age of fourteen
though, my "banker" side must have kicked in, as I started to think

about the need for a better (well, not better, just something that gave me a certificate) education. I looked at my future and decided that I would need at some point a good education that included a college degree. I was not going to get that at the performing arts school. Conversely, I was not going to get my creative side sated at a regular high school. The banker won out, and I left performing arts school to get the required qualifications to go to college. Cut to years and a business and finance certificate later, I even did the ultimate banker move and took a job at a bank. An actual bank. The "banker" became a banker.

While I quite enjoyed the numbers and analytics of working at a bank, my innovator side went MIA. It led to increasing dissatisfaction with my career and resulted in my leaving and pursuing a social sciences degree, centered around media studies, writing, and a lot of history classes. Cut, again, to several years later, and I found myself once more in the business world. This time though I was at company that was still growing, with plenty of opportunities to develop new ideas and goals. I worked initially in the international department and eventually oversaw the company's global sales units and marketing department. Neill the banker was happy with the analytics of budget projections and strategic measurements. Neill the innovator was happy with the opportunity to explore new growth opportunities with new teams. When the culture at that company changed and running the business became purely a numbers game though, the needs of my innovator side were once again left unmet. The new company culture was getting as cold as an Antarctic winter. I could not stand it. Like Shackleton and his team, I could feel forces all around the ship slowly crushing it, and I could see what was going to happen. So I followed in my hero's footsteps, got off the ship, and stepped out onto an uncertain and unpredictable future. Sadly, unlike Shackleton, I felt I had deserted my team. My hero had shown me again what an amazing leader he truly was.

My point to my brief autobiography is to show that being a banker/ innovator was not something that I practiced into because I thought it was a skill requirement of my job. It was not something I was taught in a course. It was just something I always was. Knowing that my traits were natural to me and that I had real needs to be satisfied was a powerful, eye-opening event. The knowledge gave me the confidence to be who I was in the workplace, regardless of how strange this choice would appear to others.

In the process of reflection, you might realize that leadership is really not in your DNA. Here is the kicker. Your boss probably already knows that, and your team probably already knows that. Additionally it is probably not your fault. Convention, after all, more than likely put you in the leadership role. So you need to be honest with your boss and your team as well as yourself. Not everybody is cut out to be the next American Idol, and not everybody has what it takes to be a leader, despite what some leadership books and courses promise.

According to some books I have read all you need to do to achieve greatness is follow some formula of predetermined processes and accumulate a certain set of business skills. Easy, right? Well, news flash. In the same way that not everybody can be a National Football League quarterback or that next American Idol, not everybody is cut out to be a great leader. A leader? Sure. A great leader? No.

I appreciate this thinking goes against the prevailing social convention that says you can be whatever you want to be. But the truth is you cannot be something just because you really want to be something. You can try and work hard, but if something is not in your DNA, then it's just not in your DNA. If you were the coach of an NFL team, would you play Kelly Clarkson as your starting QB even if she really, really, wanted to? I am guessing no, you wouldn't, even if she sang her heart out.

In the same way Ms. Clarkson would struggle in the NFL, leaders who are being conditioned to be something they are not also struggle. In the process of the struggle they end up being far removed from what any moderate employee would call good leadership. My unconventional norm says you should be the type of leader you are naturally gifted and inclined to be, not the type of leader convention, or your boss, says you should be. Yet many courses that we are sent to attempt to do the opposite.

Some of the courses I attended included character trait tests. These personality tests are used to determine "gaps" we have between our natural style and a predetermined, conventional, required style. Our challenge is to bridge that gap in order to become great leaders. In trying to close the gap, the result for many leaders is increased stress and self-doubt brought about by attempting to be something they are not. As a consequence, that stress and self-doubt is reflected in their leadership. This attempted personality change in turn affects their team, and not in a positive way. In my experience the stress to become something they are not causes the leaders to start to manage everything. And I mean everything. They become so paranoid about something going wrong or displeasing their boss, they micromanage every assignment and every task. Their team members start to believe they are not trusted or respected. Slowly members of the team disengage. Tasks get done haphazardly or are not completed. Rather than being proactive, team members become stagnant and wait for tasks to be assigned. Forget about creativity. That has left the building. Worst of all, eventually the good members of the team leave. Suddenly the leaders find themselves in a perpetual loop of stress, overwork, and late or failed tasks. Time does not just become a luxury; it becomes nonexistent. Yet being a leader, even a good leader, really is not that complicated, and avoiding the dreaded loop is relatively simple.

Being who you are will probably be a lot less stressful for you and your team. Team members already know your strengths and weaknesses, and they don't expect perfection from you. But they do expect leadership. So if you are a builder, go build, and if you are merchant, go sell. Just remember that those aspects of you are innate and require to be given life. But also know that like every other aspect of us, your innateness is not perfect and will come with limitations. There are times in your leadership that will call for a banker head and not an innovator one. Know that. But do not change who you are. It is not worth the stress, to anyone.

Even going through a process of self-reflection, some leaders, like Scott, will still be inclined to travel the traditional route. Your motivations will still be driven by some type of material gain, and your inspirations might remain people who have achieved great wealth or power. And there is nothing wrong with that. It is the conventional dream we are taught to aspire to. But there are many of us who have differing aspirations and relate more to the people-first approach of Amundsen or Shackleton and who want to choose an alternative pathway. It is the confidence in believing there is a different leadership road, as well as knowing and understanding yourself, that will embolden you to defy convention and be the type of leader you are naturally inclined to be.

It is highly unlikely (ok, it is impossible) that you will lead a team of people who have exactly the same motivations, inspirations, or natural style as you. There will be merchant/bankers, innovator/builders, builder/bankers, innovator/merchants, etc. Your job as a leader is not to change who they naturally are, but rather to understand them, guide and teach them, engage them, and empathize with the way they are doing things. Without empathy you will not be able to understand your team's attitude and style in a genuine manner, and as a result you will not successfully be able to undertake the next part of the unconventional leadership revolution. Know that you probably will be able to guide and engage with your team, but you will not be able to authentically motivate and inspire your team unless you know who you are and, perhaps more importantly, who they are.

Whatever motivates or inspires you, whatever type of leader you are, you must be capable of empathy. You must be capable of comprehending a member of your team's experiences and feelings. You cannot theoretically or literally have a people-first attitude or be a people-first leader without it. Empathy isn't knowing everything about someone; it is about comprehending his or her actions. If you cannot do that, none of what follows in the rest of this book will probably make any sense to you or have any real, lasting impact. Soon the book will move from "understanding you" to "leading your team." So as part of knowing yourself, think honestly about how empathetic you really are and how much empathy you really can have.

Your time is limited, so don't waste it living someone else's life. Don't be trapped by dogma, which is living with the results of other people's thinking. Don't let the noise of other's opinions drown out your own inner voice. And most important, have the courage to follow your heart and intuition.

—STEVE JOBS

4. Fears and Bravery

Conventions, in most cases, are not laws, especially in the business world. They are accepted standards or norms. Being unconventional though is not a free pass to break laws, industry compliance, or codes of conduct, or to simply do whatever you want. That isn't being unconventional. That is being foolish and probably criminal.

What unconventional behavior does is challenge the accepted standards and question normality. To do so requires us to be able to both recognize what is keeping us from being the leader we want to be, and then be confident enough to take action. In my experience it is fear that keeps us from reaching our potential and a lack of bravery that prevents us from doing anything about it.

Firsts for many of us can be awkward and uncomfortable. Your first day of school. Your first date. Your first steps on a frigid continent. Even your first attempt at writing a book. Often your first day in a new job can be as equally uncomfortable. But eventually your surroundings become familiar, you make friends, your fears subside, and things don't seem as awkward anymore.

Your first day as a leader though is usually different. If you are like me, and most employees in a supervisory role I know, your first foray into leadership will be at the place where you have worked for some time. The surroundings are familiar and you already know the people. But this is still a transition and there is still fear. To overcome the fear we make one of two choices: we give in to it and act like a conventional leader or we act with a brave, independent spirit that propels us, our team, and our organization forward.

FEAR

In a new role, our natural inclination is to not rock the boat. We want to put our stamp on a role, but we also know that making too many changes too soon is generally considered a workplace faux pas. We are new after all. What got us into the role to begin with was our technical proficiency and drive, not our leadership. We need to learn about leadership first and we know that will come from watching and learning from others.

That there is so much convention in the workplace and that there is also so much convention among leaders is not really a surprise. Being conventional is after all, well, the accepted convention. So almost immediately we end up adopting the conventions of the leaders around us. Our internal "proactive" button that helped fuel our drive gets reset. We happily implement and adopt the tasks and ideas assigned to us, or at least pretend to, as we want to show that we are team players now—even if we weren't entirely team players before. We know what is expected of us and we deliver, obligingly and with reverence to our more experienced peers. We want, if not need, their acceptance, advice, and support, and we fear doing something that will lose it.

There are few people who proceed up the corporate ladder without also pleasing their boss. You could leave your present company and take a more senior role somewhere new. You could get lucky, especially at a growing company, where new opportunities might be created and fall into your lap. (Though rare, this does happen. I speak from experience here.) But most often there is an inherent need to make sure we keep our boss happy. We know this, consciously or not. I mean, your boss probably was the person who promoted you to a leadership role to begin with. Conventionally, you kind of owe him or her, and you know that. Your boss knows it. Fear of losing the boss's approval is pervasive. I am sure you have heard of the proverb that goes "the nail that sticks out gets hammered." It is generally taught to us as a warning to not stand out or else face the hammer, or in the case of the workplace, the ax. With conformity a known and desired quality, the pressure is on new leaders to not stick out. None of us want a target on our back or to feel like we are being bullied, so we fear doing something that draws attention to us. We choose to not stick out and go along with the crowd.

Doing something new is inherently scary. There is nothing unconventional in the fear of the unknown. As a leader, new or not, there is a high likelihood that there are several layers of leadership between you and the most senior executives of the company. As a result you know there is certain information that you will remain unaware of. While not knowing what is going on at the top end of your company likely won't induce an acute bout of paranoia, it does seem to prevent us from focusing any further than an approved budget plan lets us. Fear of not wanting to be out of step with the company may be a crutch, but it is a crutch we lean on a lot.

Let's get real. Most of the fear we have in the workplace concerns what would happen if we were to lose favor with the boss. In our heads we know losing favor with the boss means the possibility of losing our job. In some cases, sadly, it probably does; such is the case of the culture of some organizations. The fear of losing our job in which we have already invested much time and effort, keeps us conforming. But are those fears genuine? Of course. Do any us really believe that the best strategy for avoiding a mistake or a bad decision is to just do what we are told and not make any big decisions? Of course not. Making mistakes and bad decisions is inevitable in your professional career as much as in your personal life. Yet the fear of getting a decision wrong or making a mistake or looking foolish or costing the company money or not getting the approval of our peers or jeopardizing our future career gives us only a false sense of security that losing favor with the boss won't eventually happen anyway. Whether you are unconventional or not.

BRAVERY

Some of you may be thinking of times when you wondered why a standard was what it was, but you didn't think much more about it. Or why you succumbed to a normal workplace rule that seemed pointless or outdated. Taking the first steps toward being unconventional and challenging standards and norms can be difficult for many of us, and it requires getting out of our comfort zone and displaying a trait that is often found lacking in the workplace: bravery.

Change is hard. Change while you are used to following conventional rules of career management? Still hard. Dealing with fear in the workplace? Easy. You do nothing. Or at least you just do what you are told to do. That's the easiest way to deal with it. Or you do something else, something more unconventional, something brave.

Throughout history we have always admired acts that required courage. Whether it is standing up to a dictatorial regime, overcoming seemingly insurmountable obstacles, or venturing into uncharted territory. Seeing others being heroic instills in us a sense of awe. Now think of your heroes at the workplaces of your career. Still thinking? Thought of someone yet, perhaps a few people? Okay, now write in their name or names in the space below:

_____

I am sure you can come up with a few names, and I am sure they all share some common characteristics. One of those traits is probably that they were unconventional, even if you did not know that label applied. During my year of being lost, I had the good fortune to meet a genuine, brave, business hero. He is a person whose name I would happily write into the above space. His name was Robert Pritzker, and he was without a doubt a successful and unconventional leader.

Robert Pritzker had successfully managed first the Marmon Group and then Colson Associates, a large group of individual companies with disparate locations and industry focuses. I first met Robert (Bob) Pritzker during the fall of 2002. A friend had provided the opportunity for me to meet with Bob, and I flew to Chicago on a red-eye from Oregon for an informal, early morning interview. It was a difficult time for both of us, so the timing was not ideal. I had been struggling to determine where I was going and what I wanted to do. Bob was in the media spotlight after a tabloid news story had been printed about a personal family matter. It was under these awkward circumstances that our paths crossed for the first time.

As I made my way up the elevator and toward the Marmon offices, I was extremely nervous. You know, that "I could throw up at any moment" type of nervousness. It might have been because of the wretched free breakfast provided at the hotel, but I knew it was due to anxiety. It was a cold, cold Chicago day, but I was sweating. I was feeling like I couldn't catch my breath. I had never met anyone of Bob's stature before, and I was intimidated. After entering the offices, I was greeted with a smile by the welcoming office assistant and offered a coffee. I said yes even though I knew that caffeine was not going to help one bit with my nerves, or the sweating. After a few moments I was taken back to Bob's office where a beaming, distinguished man in an ordinary suit put out his hand to shake mine. "Care for anything?" he asked me. While I was desperate to say some Pepto-Bismol and deodorant, I just smiled back and showed him my still hot cup of coffee.

At the start of our conversation, Bob asked me about my studies, my upbringing in Australia, what I liked about the United States, and my hopes for the future. I was pleasantly stunned. Here was a man who was running companies all over the world, who was under what must have been difficult personal circumstances, and he was getting to know me. Me, a person recently graduated with a social sciences degree with no real proven business acumen. Hardly future leaders of America potential, at least on paper. But that was exactly what he was doing. Bob was trying to find out who I was as a person. He was trying to decide if I had the potential, the ability, to be a leader. Maybe not today, maybe not tomorrow, but at some point in the future. Bob valued technical ability, but above that he valued attitude, he valued courage, and he valued humanness. His questions during our conversation were to uncover those values and attributes, not my Excel proficiencies.

After about an hour, our conversation ended. Bob thanked me (he thanked me!) for coming to Chicago and meeting with him. He told me he would do what he could to help me realize my goals. I walked out of the offices, went down the elevator, and out into the still cold Chicago air. I spotted a Starbucks, walked in, and went straight to the bathroom. Then, finally, I exhaled and breathed a sigh of relief and promptly changed my sweat coated shirt.

While it took some time and a year of business classes, eventually I found myself working for one of Bob's companies. It was during that time that I really got to know Bob the leader and Bob the man. The two were never mutually exclusive. My time working for Bob though was all too short. He sadly passed away in 2011. Even up until his last year he remained engaged in the company.

As a leader, Bob was far more interested in the products people were developing or the new markets his teams were adding than numbers. Financials were the byproduct of strategy and not the other way around. When you talked with Bob, you walked away feeling like you knew more than you started because talking with him was like having a real two-way conversation, filled with advice and guidance.

His book *Thoughts on Management* is significantly shorter than any other management book I have ever seen, yet it is filled with more tangible advice than any of them, including this one.

Bob had a simple philosophy on how companies should be run. In his book and in corporate policy books, he made it clear that while profit was a priority, it should always take a bronze medal, placing third after people and the planet. His companies complied with those priorities because he encouraged them to. And he led by example. During my last visit to the corporate offices, I had the pleasure of going into a room dedicated to preserving his memory and legacy. On one of the shelves was an award Bob had received for ethics in business. It had been given to Bob over twenty-fives year earlier, long before ethical behavior was considered a business advantage or simply part of corporate strategy. He was a pioneer, a gentleman, and a hero. He was not foolish. He was brave. Bob was the first unconventional leader I had ever met.

For all the reasons to fear being unconventional, there is only one antidote needed: bravery. Instead of fearing that you may get a decision wrong or make a mistake, be realistic and know that you will. Own it, learn from it, and become a better leader because of it. Be brave in acknowledging your shortcomings rather than looking for excuses for them. Instead of obsessing about monthly financials or sales to budget targets, focus primarily on your people and their engagement and their concerns. Be brave in placing your trust in their ability and their potential. Do not keep quiet because business political expediency expects and dictates you should. Be brave and speak your thoughts out loud. Don't accept conventional norms of hierarchical counsel. Be brave and open up your team of closest confidants and thought leaders to a circle of differing opinions and ideas, from multiple levels of management. Don't focus your team on day-to-day, metric-driven outcomes. Be brave and allow them to look forward so they can plan and achieve goals ahead of their time. Do what you can for your team without thinking about what they can do for you. It was Robert Pritzker's way. It is an unconventional way.

Convention, we think, acts like a shield that protects us from blame and sometimes responsibility. When you follow convention and make a mistake or a poor decision, you can point to convention as the culprit. You were just doing what your company expected you to do. It shields us from our sense of personal identity and as a result protects us from having to take personal responsibility. It acts like a dam against alternative and progressive attitudes to keep us from moving forward. While surely a coincidence, there is some irony in fear being a four-letter word starting with "f." Nothing can mess us up more, both personally and professionally, than fear. Perhaps more than anything else, fear is what could derail your plans to be unconventional, no matter how genuine your intentions are. Learning to let go of the fear will be perhaps, for some of you anyway, your biggest challenge in becoming an unconventional leader. Recognize the fear. Acknowledge the fear. Forget the fear. Be brave and act with courage. It could well be the single most liberating thing you do in your professional career. This will be challenging, I know. So when you start to doubt your ability to get rid of the fear do the following:

1. Remember, throughout history there have been a lot of people who have done things a lot braver with a lot more to lose.
2. Think about the person whose name you wrote in the blank earlier in this chapter. Why was that person a hero to you? How do you think he or she might have been unconventional? Do you think he or she would let go of the fear?
3. Visualize again what your ideal workplace looks like.

A stress ball and a Twix bar might work too. But also remember that nobody ever said it would be easy. Whichever leadership pathway you choose will have hurdles. It's so much easier to overcome them when you are not afraid.

All your efforts to overcome fear and act with bravery will be undone if you continue to adopt conventions that have the opposite effect and only add to a negative culture. As a result it is important to recognize, understand, and change when your behavior could be installing fear in others.

As a call to action, this book illustrates a way for leaders to create both a positive and productive working environment, as well how to have meaningful and impactful relationships with their boss and team members. To achieve that desired outcome, you are starting to learn how to adopt a new people-focused approach and to let go of the many existing leadership conventions. You should be aware that some of the conventions help to keep a culture of fear and anxiety within an organization. One of those conventions is the leadership hammer.

Along with having duties and responsibilities, a leader also has certain workplace authorities. Depending on the level of leadership (executive, director, manager, etc.), the more expansive the workplace authorities leaders have. They may have the authority to fire, hire, and "retire" some employees. They may also have the authority to delegate and pontificate. Some may get the opportunity to sit in a fancy office and expense those Monday morning lattes. As part of their authorities, leaders by convention also get a mythical hammer. It is a symbol of authority that metaphorically appears in the top drawer of the desk in that fancy office. It is an intangible symbol of authority that everyone knows exists. What we don't know is whether leaders will use it or not. And if they do, how and when it will be used. Not knowing creates a culture of fear and paranoia. It is the culture where the ego-driven, hammer-in-hand leader thrives.

Any additional authorities that leaders receive can fuel the flames of an already festering ego fire. They turn once cordial and friendly supervisors into prima donna managers. The new authorities result in a new attitude. Suddenly, with a new title, they know everything about everything, including the rules of acceptable behavior and fairness. They believe that team members should know exactly what they are thinking, all the time. They know that everyone knows they have a mythical hammer. One out-of-turn remark, one slight mistake, one minute late to the office, and that hammer can come out.

Now think about what that hammer represents. It stands for the ability to exert authority. It is a symbol of toughness and, dare I say it, manliness. It says I don't take any nonsense from anyone. More than anything it is a conduit of fear. Conventional leaders like fear. They think it is what keeps their employees doing their job. Except they are wrong. Their teams may get the tasks done in the short term, but they do them without inspiration and without passion. In being treated like robots long term, the employees become robots without soul or spirit. What the hammer really says to team members is that they have a leader who cannot be bothered to take the time to actually think about why a mistake happened or care enough to ask someone why they were one minute late. Having a hammer is so predictable, so conventional, and oh so pointless. As a convention, you can touch this.

Along with increased authorities leaders also have choices. They can choose to set aside any preconceived and conventional ideas about being a leader. They can choose to be people focused and still be successful. In choosing to be a people-first leader, they can get rid of the hammer. And the carrot. And the stick. (Another one of those conventional and oh so droll leadership buzz terms.) They don't need any of those things because they practice the philosophy that an engaged, motivated, and inspired team will be its own hammer (or carrot or stick). They know that mistakes in the workplace happen and that they can actually be positive learning experiences. They know that as leaders they also have a responsibility for those mistakes. They know that a positive work climate is far more beneficial to producing results than an environment of fear. And if tough love is needed, they know there are better tools to use than one that, if used incorrectly, can leave messy holes in the wall and in their team. No time should be hammer time.

The hammer is an archaic relic of leadership past that deserves to be consigned to the workshop, not the top drawer of a desk. People-focused leaders bury it. They don't need it. They don't need a culture of fear. Instead they engage their team in a positive and supportive manner and in the process also get rid of their own fears of making mistakes. They talk openly and honestly and not behind closed doors with occasional stare downs. They are understanding and empathetic, not authoritarian and demanding. Being authoritarian and demand-ing is ultimately what that metaphorical hammer represents. You know it, and your team knows it. But people-focused unconventional leaders should keep a real hammer handy. That "world's best boss" certificate is not going to hang itself.

There are many things we cannot change about our working conditions. As much as we would like to, it is unlikely you will get approval to move your cubicle to the sunnier climate of a beach condo in Maui. Trust me, I tried. But the silver lining of fear is that it is a condition we can change. It is a change worth making. You just have to be brave enough.

How wonderful it is that nobody need wait a single
moment before starting to improve the world.
—ANNE FRANK

5. Eat, Live, Pray, and Inspire

It would be great if most of us were inspired on some level to go to work because, like the basset hound from an earlier chapter, we want to please somebody. The reality for most of us though is that much more mundane motivations keep us going to work, while a lack of inspiration makes us want to avoid jumping the hurdle that is our morning commute.

Employees are usually motivated to go to work because they need food to eat and a place to live. Going to work and receiving a paycheck allows them to satisfy those needs. When we do not feel like going to work, it is not because we are not motivated (we still need food and a place to live), it is because we are not inspired. Sadly, a focus on leaders providing inspiration in the workplace can be pretty unconventional and, in my observations, all too rare.

Motivations and inspirations affect a person's desire and willingness to do something, his or her attitude. In the workplace we hear a lot about motivations, especially during compensation times. But when was the last time you heard leaders at your workplace talk about inspiration? If you have, you are one of the fortunate ones. I have been lucky, having managed to find inspiration in places, people, and events that others have never thought twice about. It therefore has been a huge surprise to me that so many leaders I have known or worked with have no insight into what actually inspires them, let alone think that they have a duty and responsibility to inspire others. Conventional wisdom in the workplace seems to be to motivate. I say inspire, then motivate, but then inspire again.

As you already know, I have turned repeatedly to the great polar explorers of the early twentieth century to find my inspiration and twenty-first-century leadership style. Amundsen's efforts in leading the first group of human beings to set foot on the South Pole, with organizational excellence and speed, was an achievement of global significance. Shackleton faced an almost impossible situation yet overcame the most confounding obstacles to lead all of his men to safety in a story that continues to astound and inspire. Scott's heroic legacy enthralled a faltering empire, and his contribution to the scientific studies left an equally indelible impression. They are all different men, with differing leadership styles and differing motives, which is why, to me, they all make interesting leadership case studies.

The last manager I worked for was clearly inspired by his religious faith. Because the company was not a religious organization, it must have been difficult for him to demonstrate inspiration to his subordinates without using the very thing that seemed to hearten him the most. But to his credit, he did find ways. The ways he chose were neither overtly religious in nature nor particularly obviously inspirational, even if the results sometimes were to me. One example was particularly inspiring to me, though I do not believe it was intentionally used for that purpose, but rather as a lesson, with a planned outcome of gained knowledge.

At a typical meeting, my boss handed out a book to my peers and me. As an ongoing exercise, we were to read a chapter and then discuss it as a group the following week. A corporate book club as it were. The book in question was *The World's Most Powerful Leadership Principle: How to Become a Servant Leader* by James C. Hunter. There are many books on this particular subject, and a quick scan of the book covers would reveal that some of them are quite obviously religious in nature. This one is not, though once you start reading the book, the text clearly follows along the lines of the teachings of Jesus Christ, with "do unto others as you would have them do onto you" a particularly resonating theme. For my boss, this was a great book for him to share in order to demonstrate what has inspired him. Even though I am not particularly religious, I found the book to be, well, really quite inspiring.

The reading of the book also involved also having to do a task. As a result, over time the inspirational core started to become lost as I tried to figure out what the action item was in the reading each and every week. Eventually even I started to focus less on the inspirational nature of the book and mostly viewed it like a teaching session in college, with knowledge to be learned and then to be tested on, if not completely applied. It no longer became about my boss imparting inspiration but rather about whether or not I was motivated to do a task and pass the test.

Being inspirational is really not about what you make other people do. It is about what you do. And trying to be inspirational can as a result be challenging for all leaders. Some people will find what you do inspiring and others will not. I have failed myself once or twice myself to be inspiring. I did though learn the lesson of acting inspiring, eventually. But not until after a few failed attempts.

Each year I would take my team on a team-building event, a pretty conventional workplace staple. This particular year, my goal was to inspire the team to work together to complete goals. Incidentally I had failed the year before in this particular goal, even though I had used "finding your inspiration" as the theme of the team-building event. C'est la vie! But I digress. This team-building event took place at a zip lining adventure park. The first part of the event was led by an adventure park instructor, who set up some challenging, obstacle-style goals that required the team to work together in order to complete. The second part of the event was the more fun zip lining through the trees, which required absolutely no team effort whatsoever.

Because the team members had different experience and skill levels with zip lining (some had never done it before), what I hoped was that the lessons of the first part of the day would inspire the team to work together and help each other, especially those with no experience or skills, during the second part of the day. While the first part of the day got off to a shaky start, eventually the team began communicating effectively enough and working together well enough to complete the obstacle goals. Success! Then came the second part. I held back to watch as team members began the tree zip lining, seeing if they would work together or not. The answer was obvious very quickly and was an adamant no. The skilled and experienced zip liners were gone in a flash while the less skilled and experienced struggled toward the back. Total failure. At the time for me, epic failure.

At first I blamed the leaders among the team for the failure. How could they have not seen my obvious intentions? After one of my trusted leaders, who I respected and admired greatly, calmed me down and pulled me off the proverbial business place ledge, I reflected on my own mistakes during the day. One major mistake was particularly clear. My problem was that my intentions, to inspire teamwork, were not that obvious, because I had not done any of the inspiring. I had passed over my inspirational duties to a complete stranger. Inspiration remember is not an assigned to task to your team, it is a duty you have.

It would have been an easy mistake to avoid if I had just recalled the actions of the people who had inspired me, the polar explorers. Had either Amundsen or Shackleton been the leader at that team event, there is no doubt in my mind that they would not have left the first part of the day up to an instructor who was a stranger to my team. Amundsen, especially, would have probably gone to the adventure park earlier, possibly many times, been trained on the team-building events, and been coached on how to guide the team toward success. At the event he would have been the one doing the instructing, not the adventure park employee. In leading his team to the South Pole, there is no way that Amundsen would have left inspirational responsibilities to a stranger, and I should not have left my responsibilities to someone else.

I could blame the lack of inspirational convention in the workplace on my team-building mistake. But that would be just an excuse, and as an unconventional leader, I know better. I simply forgot what inspires me and that it isn't enough to just know what inspires you. You have to use that knowledge too, and in doing so, you will act in ways that inspire others.

After the team-building failure and my "come to Amundsen" moment, I refocused my efforts to inspire so I could not shirk my inspirational duties. An opportunity presented itself soon after when an employee from another department came to me with an idea for the company to focus more concretely on socially responsible platforms. The company had always been involved with charitable donations and some community activities, but never under an umbrella of an organized and systematic program. The employee showed me some literature that indicated companies with socially responsibility programs were outperforming competitors with no such programs. My compassionate side was intrigued, and my business side thought this made good commercial sense. My leadership side saw this as an opportunity.

I presented the idea of a social responsibility program to the executive team and fought hard for approval. I would not be taking no for an answer. Once I gained approval, I proceeded to form a cross-functional team to create the social responsibility program for the company, with me acting as the executive sponsor. No more outside instructor this time. I was going to be the person demonstrating how to clear the obstacles, and I did. Within two years the social responsibility team was a visible presence in the company, along with an associate-formed green team. They achieved a great deal (and hopefully still are). It was not my hard work that led to the success of the team though; it was the hard work of the people on the team. They had found something that inspired them in working for a company with social compassion. They knew that my support for the team was unwavering. I was very proud to be a part of giving them that inspiration and support. It was, to use a business cliché, a win-win.

After two years, the social responsibility team was given the honor of presenting its work at a companywide meeting. All the team members were acknowledged and given a reward. Well, all except one: me. My boss had asked that my name and picture be removed from the companywide presentation. I do not know why. I was demonstrating and living the ethos of servant leadership as well as I knew how. Having an executive, visibly and tangibly involved in a team like this, could have potentially inspired other employees to get involved. It demonstrated that the company's leaders were committed to the values of the employees in a real, meaningful, relatable way. I think, though, that convention got the better of my boss, so I could hardly fault him. Sadly that opportunity was lost, but I feel confident knowing that at least ten employees, and probably a lot more, had been genuinely inspired by my actions. I had learned from my previous mistakes and made "inspiring" an action item instead of a noun. Action is what true inspiration requires.

If I could eventually figure out this inspiration thing, so can you. So go figure out what inspires you, and go from there. Find your team members' basset hound, or Amundsen, or Shackleton. It's as simple as that. Then use that knowledge to inspire your team. You want them to come to work not because they are motivated by internal needs, but because they are inspired to do so. Right? I think, scratch that, I believe we all do.

6. Hercules and Changes

During one of my first executive leadership roles, an employee accused me of dismantling the team I had inherited. The result of the "dismantling" was a termination; his own. The employee told me that I was sacrificing him in order to put in place my own team. He was correct, but only to a point.

At first I was deeply saddened that this employee saw my actions this way. But I also understood his feelings. The team skills that I knew were needed, both now and in the future, this employee did not have and could not grasp. I had tried to give this team member the skills, spending my time educating him and sending him to courses to learn the needed skills. I utilized a disproportionate amount of my time coaching him as best as I could. In the end terminating this employee was not an easy decision.

Termination of this employee was though the right decision—for me, my team, and for him. He had tried very hard to learn and grasp the needed skills, but they did not come so easily to him. He was an engineer, defying nature by being in sales management. I could not risk the future success of my team and had to make the tough decision. That was the only termination I made, and it was done only after a long period of trying to help the employee defy nature. The rest of the team were not defying anything, and while many, like me, were relatively inexperienced, I knew I had a responsibility to let them grow. They had the DNA needed, and I wanted the best possible team of eager-to-learn, proactive employees to take with me on what I hoped would be a safe, meaningful journey for all.

Most leaders inherit a team over which they had little control in creating. As a result, most of us are probably going to have to make some changes at some point in time. Now I am not saying all new leaders should go out and fire their entire new team. Far from that. I'm saying, if the team is not adequately equipped to do the needed job then create a plan to changes things. Those changes rarely, if ever, have to include terminating people and hiring new ones. Most often it just means a possible realignment of duties and roles or a potential organizational structure change. To make any changes possible means working with your boss and your human resources team to get the team dynamics right.

But before you go chatting with your recruitment personnel, you need to do a very important if sometimes unconventional task first. That task is to thoroughly understand the technical and behavioral skills that your team has and needs. Doing this is critical to a people-first leader because it allows you to get to know your team, to continually engage with your team, and most importantly, to grow with your team. Even if you are not a new leader, an ongoing skills assessment of your team is important because priorities change, goals change, and people's motivations change.

To the pole! Excluding the scientific portion of Scott's South Pole adventure, the strategic goals of Amundsen and Scott were essentially the same: be the first to lead a team to reach the South Pole and safely return home. As we know, the outcomes for the two teams were tragically different. Both men's leadership styles had got their respective teams to the pole, yet one team returned safely home while the other perished. The lesson we can all learn from the South Pole race is that your leadership style can only get you so far along the path to a strategic destination. No matter how well you know yourself or how inspired you are, what gets you safely to complete your strategic goal journey is also having a skilled team. A team not afraid to speak up. A team engaged in the journey. A team motivated and inspired to do the hard work.

Let's be honest here. You may have thought after the first few chapters of this book that it's all about you. Well, it isn't all about you, and don't say I didn't warn you. It certainly starts with you, but a start is after all just the beginning. Your team will be doing the navigating, laying the food stores, taking care of the dogs, and all the hard lifting, sledging, and hauling. Unless you're Hercules and you can do everything yourself, having the right team is, unquestionably, critical. Therefore your team members' skills, their drive, and their attitude are all very important. You, as their leader, will most certainly influence all of those needed factors. As a result one of your biggest challenges as a transformative leader is getting the balance of your team right. It is the difference between success and failure. Your actions and choices are critically important.

Back to the South Pole. Amundsen chose to surround himself with a team of highly skilled individuals in specialized areas. Shackleton similarly surrounded himself with a team straight out of a polar exploration fantasy league. But for the extraordinary navigational skills of Frank Worsley, Shackleton's captain on *Endurance*, it is quite likely that there would be no great survival story to tell. Scott chose people he could trust, who "looked" liked explorers, and who shared a similar understanding of the hierarchical type of leadership he was familiar with, ensuring they would be, without question, loyal to him. In the business world, we should probably call Robert Scott's team-creating approach what it is, "ego-nepotism." It's an all-too-typical standard:

hire and surround yourself with people you trust because they think and act like you, have an unquestioned loyalty to you, and will do what you ask of them without ever challenging your decisions. Does it work? Maybe. Scott did get to the South Pole. Does it create the best possible exploration team and ensure success beyond one part of the strategic journey? Probably not. Just because you think employees look like they have skills, it does not mean they do. You need to do more work than just judge a person's abilities by a look or a feeling.

But, Neill, haven't my employees already been hired, by convention, for their skills and technical ability? Yes, they probably were. But don't people change? Don't their needs and career goals change? And was your team's emotional balance ever evaluated as part of the hiring? Plus, when was the last time you, in conjunction with your team members, did a skills analysis? When was the last time you even did one on yourself? When was the last time you even communicated to your team, as a whole, what skills you thought were needed or what skills the team thought were needed? This is a simple exercise to undertake yet one, in my experience, that rarely happens, at least not in the required depth.

It is hard to imagine that Amundsen would have ever reached the pole if one of his team was consistently complaining about how much weight he was pulling, or the cold, or the diet. Skills should be determined from the perspective that both an emotional intelligence skill set and a technical ability skill set will be required. Seriously, when was the last time you purposely hired the constant complainer, the neurotic gossiper, or the person who yelled all the time? I have. You probably have. Why? Because we did not take into account the need for an emotional balance within our team. I get it. In the workplace it is difficult for many to talk about emotional intelligence, at least face-to-face. Additionally convention generally gets the better of us, and we hire the most experienced and technically qualified, even if we have doubts about the candidates' emotional intelligence. But there are courses available that evaluate our emotional skills. Utilize the courses, and here is the important part: use the information.

Skipping forward, you have done your skills analysis and have determined that you do need to make some changes. Perhaps a termination? Perhaps a new position? Perhaps a change in duties? Now what? Well, there are a number of obstacles you are going to have overcome in order to have your team built for success. But let's look at recruiting, because generally this is the most cumbersome. Plus the other changes usually follow a similar path.

Conventional hiring usually involves a recruiter, perhaps a few of your peers, and you. Some leaders open up the hiring process to their entire team, and I certainly give kudos to those who do so for their all-inclusive approach. But unless your recruiter, your peers, and in some cases, your entire team understand exactly the skill set required, they probably are going to be more emotional recruiters than practical ones. Not that there is anything wrong with emotion, but we are talking about the best possible team here, not the one that makes everyone feel good. Recruiting for a great team, after all, requires a level head. It is with a level head that you are going to have to approach your first hurdle: your boss. If you are one of a fortunate minority to have a high-trust relationship with your boss, this step is probably going to be relatively pain free. Given that your boss has probably just hired you into your leadership role, there is a good chance that you have some goodwill already banked with him or her. My recommendation is to use that goodwill now in building your team. The goodwill will not last forever.

For argument's sake, let's say your boss is not new, the goodwill is depleted, and there is not a high-trust relationship in place. Now what? Well, you are going to have to be well prepared with a solid argument, with a focus on strategic destination and why you need to make the changes you want. Nobody wants to listen to a person argue for change for the sake of change without any tangible benefit to the organization. It is to that last point (tangible benefit) that you should focus. Your boss wants the organization to succeed in the short and long term so he or she will be open to hearing about your proposed changes. A word of warning though: leave emotion at your boss's doorway. It will not help, nor should it. If your boss approves your changes from an emotional perspective, he or she is doing it to make you feel good or to get you out of his or her office. Remember, recruiting, or any team change, requires a level head, not an emotional one. If your boss does not approve your changes, do not give up. Repeat. Do not give up. I am not suggesting you verbally beat your boss into submission. Rather I am suggesting you ask him or her the direct question: what will it take to get the changes approved? It's a pretty simple question really and one that is worth focusing your time on, even if your immediate reaction is to think that your boss is an idiot. Once bosses have the answers they need, it will be very hard for them to not approve changes.

The next hurdle will be your human resources department, or rather the conventional recruiting practices you and your HR department probably engage in. Conventional recruiting goes something like this:

A. Post the job vacancy internally and online, with required education and experience, and the request for all interested applicants to send in a resume and cover letter.
B. An HR department associate reviews (I use that term loosely) applicant materials, searching for key buzzwords that indicate the candidate has the required qualifications and experience.
C. Acceptable applicants are sent to you to choose from, generally after conducting a phone interview and then an in-person interview.

It is at point B that the biggest conflicts between hiring manager and recruiter should occur, yet they rarely do. I do not use the term "conflict" as a negative either. Conflict is good. Your recruiter is your ally and is there to help you. As a hiring manager, you should be having open and honest conversations with the recruiter about the type of candidate you are seeking. If you tell your recruiter you need this experience with this education, guess what? He or she is going to send you candidates with that experience and that education.

Your biggest obstacle to creating the best possible team, therefore, is not your boss or your human resources department; it is you. Yes, you. Or rather it is the fact you have adopted the conventional recruiting philosophy that says you need to hire candidates with this education and that experience. Newsflash: you don't. Second newsflash: you probably shouldn't. Your boss and your HR department are just responding to what you have told them. If you fail to communicate exactly what you need, do not get all frustrated that the recruiter did not send you the resumes you were looking for. If you failed to mention that you need somebody with future leadership potential, somebody who is outspoken, somebody who is good with dogs or can go really fast on skis, somebody who is pragmatic and can handle a turn-of-the-century navigational system, or somebody who is results driven, then guess what? You only have yourself to blame. A rule of being unconventional means you are going to have to break accepted, conventional practices, and recruiting is one of the most ingrained practices in the business world.

Having a team that is balanced both with technical ability and emotional compatibility should be the primary goal of all good leaders. No plan, no matter how well thought out, can truly succeed unless the team balance is in order. Conventional employee management often lets us down in achieving this most important of leadership goals. So it is important to think of creative and perhaps innovative ways to help you with the team balance. Seek out for alternative views and opinions. A view I like is in *Hiring for Attitude* by Mark Murphy, who makes the case for treading different recruitment ground a lot more comprehensively than I do here and, I might add, as well as any person has. It is after all your attitude and the attitude of your team that will ultimately lead to success or failure, or worse, mediocrity. Unless, of course, you have the strength of Hercules.

> There is no man so stupid that he doesn't
> have something important to say.
> —ROALD AMUNDSEN

7. Three Ds and Rs

I have always been a bit of a contemplator. It is probably the banker DNA in me. Like many people I contemplate philosophical things like why we are here, if there is a God, or why there are three hundred television channels and still nothing interesting to watch. As a result, during college I was drawn to some of the social sciences, such as philosophy and sociology. One semester I had a break in my schedule I needed to fill with a class, so I decided to take a class called Social Thought.

This particular sociology class explored how and why societies had evolved into the organized structures we see today, with a particular focus on the influence of philosophers. We had the opportunity to study John Locke, his works, and their influence on modern-day America. Of particular focus, as with most Locke studies, was the "social contract." For those unfamiliar, the social contract is (and I am paraphrasing here) the list of duties and responsibilities that a citizen has with its government and vice versa. A citizen agrees to follow government-sanctioned laws, and in return the government protects the citizens from those who don't follow the laws.

As an idea I found the social contract fascinating. I had never thought of there being some intrinsic contract between the government and me before. Specifically a contract that keep us as a social unit safe and progressing. When I became a leader, I believed that a similar, equally as informal, workplace contract was also needed. Something more than just a one-sided job description with a list of duties. A contract between a leader and his or her team. As a leader, I agree to help guide, coach, teach, engage, motivate, and inspire my employees, and in return they stay focused, committed, proactive, and dedicated to their role. It was an informal contract that for most part worked and was pretty unconventional.

I wonder if you have ever given much thought to the duties and responsibilities section of your job description document. My guess would be that you certainly read through it before taking on any role. It is effectively a contract after all, so you should read it, even the fine print. Some of you may even review it periodically with your boss. But how often do you really question or challenge the listed duties and responsibilities? If mine was like yours, it generally lists a series of expected functional management-type duties, and that is only to be expected cause thats conventionally how they are drafted. But how many of the duties or responsibilities specifically address those relating to people tasks and duties? Probably not many, even in the fine print. It just isn't the convention to do so.

An important task for all unconventional leaders should be to reevaluate your prescribed duties and responsibilities. Having the title "leader" does not just come with job-sanctioned power, it also comes with certain inherent obligations. There is an implied contract between you and your team with clear duties and responsibilities. Some are duties that should be listed on any good leadership job description, yet seldom are. Others I see as personal responsibilities that almost certainly never appear in a leadership job ad. Changing your mind-set on how you see your obligations, even if they are not listed on your job description document, which they probably aren't, will help your team cohesion and culture. It can also help set a positive attitude for the entire company.

DUTY I: KEEP YOUR TEAM ENGAGED.

You cannot know your team's abilities, feelings (yes feelings!), or what they can do and want to do unless they are—drumroll—engaged in their job and engaged with you. By now of course you have already read the previous chapter and begun the thought process on how you will go about completing a skills analysis with your team members. You need to take it further than just the skills assessment though and find out what truly motivates them and what engages them. And more importantly, what will keep them engaged. The answers they give you may surprise you. However, it is not enough to just listen to what engages your team; you need to do something with that information. And doing something really is pretty easy if you are willing to spend the time and effort.

So let's do a hypothetical. I haven't done one up to now, and while it's tempting not to start, this seems like a good place to try one out. You have an employee on your team who has a relatively junior, minimal responsibility position. The employee has always struck you as smart and capable but often seems bored and disinterested. You are sitting down with this person doing the skills analysis. During the conversation the employee reveals to you that he or she has a passion for writing (purely coincidental choice of passion there). You ask, "If your job had some writing-type tasks, would it decrease your apparent boredom and increase your engagement?" The employee says yes. You ask him or her to make a deal with you. You offer to help find some writing tasks to be included in the employee's duties. In return he or she agrees to work on that bored and disinterested look. Bam, you just made a leadership contract, and you hopefully should also have a more engaged employee. Remember though, you better follow through with finding those tasks. Don't promise what you cannot deliver.

A common frustration among employees I have worked with is the lack of perceived opportunity for career advancement. As a result they often disengage, especially the talented, capable ones. You have a duty to help the individuals within your team grow. It is not enough to know what they want to do in the future. You also have to help them be prepared for when any opportunity does present itself. They will not be able to grow unless you give them the opportunities. It is after all people who really provide opportunities, not companies. And it is leaders, good leaders, who help keep their team engaged by making sure they are equipped to take advantage of them.

DUTY 2: ACT WITH FAIRNESS.

We often in the workplace think of fairness as treating everybody the same. It is a conventional mind-set I would like you to change. Acting with fairness should be about treating everybody's "teamwork output" the same. Remember, we are all individuals, with different histories, etc. Leaders should treat us differently because we are different. Some may want extra attention and guidance. Others may prefer to be left alone. Some may be more cautious and thoughtful in their approach. Others a little more reckless. And that is okay. If you are already shaking your head at this unconventional approach, ask your team members. They know they are all different. They know they have different workloads, different tasks, and differing styles. But when it comes to team-focused goals, well, then you are all on the same page. And they know that too.

You may think your team loves hauling a hundred pounds of strategic supplies over hundreds of nautical business miles, but I guarantee they will probably hate it more if one of their peers is not pulling his or her fair share of the weight. Acting with fairness means calling the slacker out on the lack of team output, and acknowledging the effort of those who carried the extra weight left by the slacker. Should the slacker get the same reward as the star hauler? Of course not. Compensation and benefits matter, and so does your acknowledgment of their efforts, and sometimes this means the positive and negative efforts. In the "everyone's a winner" culture, I know it goes against our natural inclination to exclude slackers from team rewards, but they should be. People want to be held accountable. But more than that, they want other people held accountable to the same standard. The only way to make a standard, well, the same, is when evaluating team-focused goals and tasks.

Note: Be aware that accountability, in my experience, can be a double-edged sword. Getting the balance right can take some trial and error. Don't give up though. Tracking accountability within your team is also a pretty good people-focused metric. Just saying.

DUTY 3: BE A TEAM PLAYER, ESPECIALLY DURING ROUGH WEATHER.

Here is a personal known fact about me: I like penguins. Yes, penguins. When I decided to get a tattoo after years of hesitancy, my friends knew I would be getting one of a penguin (in a bow tie, no less) before even I did. I cannot exactly pinpoint why I have such a deep affection for the animal, but given my admiration for Antarctic explorers and my comfort in working within a team-oriented unit, the bonds between us are pretty obvious. The emperor penguin in the Antarctic is probably familiar to many of you, especially if you have seen them in movies, such as *March of the Penguins*.

For me, one of the most inspiring aspects of the emperor penguin is that during the cold winter months, they will join together, form a circle, and shield each other from the cold elements. In working together they ensure their survival through periods of extreme cold weather. Your team will experience similar periods, no matter how hard you try to shield the members from the cold. The lesson we have already learned from Robert Scott is that an ego and self-centered approach may get you to your goal, but it won't keep you warm during the bad times. If you want long-term success and survival, then check your ego and circle in with the rest of your team. Working together with your team will also provide all of you with learning and growth opportunities. Some leaders may think they know everything (and you know who you are!), and deserve to not have to bare the brunt of any bad weather, but you don't. Sorry.

RESPONSIBILITY 1: SPEAK UP AND LET YOUR TEAM DO THE SAME.

Arguably the major tragedy of Scott's fateful second polar journey was that it could have been so easily avoided. It could have been avoided simply if the culture of the exploration team had allowed for open and honest communication. Not just from within Scott's direct chain of command, but from within all levels of the group. The poorly marked and stocked food stores certainly played a part in the polar party dying (most likely from hunger) on the return from the pole. Men within Scott's team knew they had not planned the food stores well enough for a successful return journey. Yet they did not speak up despite having opportunities to do so and despite knowing the South Pole team's return journey was likely to be problematic. They may also have known, though it is only conjecture, that it might end in their death. So why did they not speak up? I believe it is because the unwritten rules of the British navy, which was heavily embedded into the Scott exhibition team culture, did not allow for open communication. It almost certainly did not encourage or condone speaking against authority. While the British navy may have thought this was a good and needed practice, it did not help save Scott's team. And it really has no place anywhere there are carpeted tiles on the floor and partitions between furniture.

Convention, like the British navy of old, still dictates that we give more reverence to the people in our team who have the most authority. As a result, leaders often only include those team members directly reporting to them in their inner circle. This convention is one I have never understood and never followed. I have always tried to include team members from multiple levels of authority in my direct team meetings, even if they were not one of my direct reports. Why? Because the more conduits and levels of communication you create within your team, the more likely you are to receive the information you need. It also sends a message that you value hearing different thoughts and ideas.

If your functional management area includes hundreds if not thousands of employees, clearly having them all attend every team meeting is simply not possible. But if you want more than a one-dimensional organizational view during your team meetings, include people from more than one level of authority in your team. It isn't conventional, but it will bring a more holistic approach to your meetings and, more importantly, will give voice to those who most often feel like they don't have one. It is also perfectly okay, if not conventional, for someone on your team to play devil's advocate, even if that person actually does agree with you. Indeed I would encourage that someone be the designated "arguer for the sake of arguing" person at every meeting. Trust me, it can't hurt. In my experience the people most likely to play devil's advocate are the team members who don't directly report to you. You aren't immune from yes-men, even in the best of team cultures. But you can mitigate the risk.

You also aren't immune from having a responsibility to lead by example. In order for your team members to speak up, you will also need to speak up. Seeing you being open and frank with your opinions and thoughts, whether to peers or your boss, will send them a clear message that you encourage open and frank opinions from them. The difficult part of this responsibility is that so many corporate cultures, while not exactly like the British navy of old, do not really encourage the type of open dialogue and dissension that should exist at every level of an organization. I cannot begin to tell you how many times I had to endure the "look". Its a look I call the stare-down virus. It's that look from a person that says be quiet. I rarely was though. I tried to not let the corporate stare-down virus get to me, but it sometimes did. I would even occasionally receive a chastising for bringing up issues that "might upset people." I still spoke up. I endured other executives talking smack about my teams. I gave the smack right back—at them, not their teams. When the corporate food supplies began to get really low, I spoke and spoke and presented and spoke. It turned out to be futile, but at least I was heard and my team knew I had spoken up. It told them I would not let the stare-down virus get to me and that they should not let it get to them.

RESPONSIBILITY 2: TAKE CARE OF YOUR PEOPLE'S HEALTH.

A good team wants to perform, but sometimes there might be a day when a few members of your team just cannot get their heads around the task at hand. Asking them, or worse, making them continue on will probably lead to frustration and stress. For you both. Do the responsible thing. Let them leave and clear their mind *before* the stress and frustration really gets to them. A change of climate might just be all they need. If your team members are like my writing technique, their best work probably happens at two in the morning when their heads are clear—or in the shower, or while walking the dog, or over a pizza with friends. It rarely happens naturally on demand, between the hours of eight and five, at a desk. Yet convention says that your team should be able to produce on a set schedule, Monday to Friday. I always preferred my team to have a clear head. If that meant leaving work at 8:05 a.m. after exactly five minutes of work, then so be it. If it meant them working from home and not coming into the office at all, then so be it. If it meant them not doing anything at all from home, then so be it. You need a stress and frustrated-free team more than you need a group of Tylenol-popping zombies sitting in cubicles producing nothing of value. So ease up, if you can, on the whole eight to five in the office thing. It will, I promise, have a positive impact on not only the attitude and work output of your team member but also on the team culture.

If you follow the duties listed previously, you will almost definitely spot opportunities to demonstrate that you care about your employees' health. Take travel, for example. If you are like how I was then you have a team that travels a lot. I traveled a lot. Believe it or not, business travel is not the glamorous lifestyle you may think it is. If you do not travel, talk to someone in your organization about the countless hours at airports, on planes, in rental cars or taxis; the nights at strange hotels with weird, uncomfortable beds and showers that take two calls to the front desk and four hours to figure out how to work; the jet lag that leaves you wide awake at 3:00 a.m.; and the time away from loved ones and the missed memories with them. Instead you have new memories you just created with some executive schmuck you would rather forget. I haven't even mentioned the food. Don't get me started on the food!

So I understood clearly the negative part of travel. So did my team and so does yours. If possible, make it as painless as you can for them to endure time away from loved ones, from their life. Let them book a recovery day with the trip. Let them book the flights they want, not the cheapest with the nine-hour layovers at three different airports. And if your organization is not permitted to fly business class, use all those miles and free upgrades you have and give them to your team. That's right, I said it. If there is an unwritten convention of the business traveler, it's that your earned miles and upgrades are to be used by you and you only. Poppycock. Share them and you will not only earn some love from your team and that "world's best boss" mug, but you actually just might help the teams physical and mental health.

Taking care of your team members' health does not just end with the physical pitfalls of air travel. It also includes doing the best you can to take care of their emotional health. Arguably the biggest threat to their emotional health is stress. You cannot eliminate all stress from an employee's life, but you can mitigate the amount of work-related stress. Great planning buys extra time, and it is worth the investment to be organized. Consequently, you should allow your team the luxury of time to also be organized. Like it will for you, being organized will allow your team the time to focus on the bigger picture. There is nothing worse than being expected to develop, implement, and manage new ideas when you are given absolutely no time to actually do anything. But when you are, the results can be extremely rewarding for you, your team, and your company. So let your team have time.

If there is one stressor I have seen that causes ill health to your team more than any other, it is the stress caused by a culture of fear. We have all probably had the experience of working for a boss who rules with an iron first and creates a climate where employees are in fear of retribution, punishment, or termination. I doubt any of us felt good working in that climate. Don't repeat it.

Before I lose you on this issue of health I know you cannot make anyone quit smoking, or start exercising, or put down that second burrito, but you can help employees take care of some of their physical and mental health. In doing so, you will have a positive impact on the company culture. When that fear-driven boss sees the positive impact your team is having, and especially how they are doing it, it might even soften them, even just a little.

RESPONSIBILITY 3: INSTILL A SENSE OF PERSONAL BELIEF.
The only thing better than believing in yourself is having someone else believe in you. If there has been one act of leadership that has meant more to me than any other, it has been to instill in my team members the confidence to undertake any task assigned and solve any problem

presented. Will team members need help? Sure, and providing help to them is, at its core, your job. It is through being available and providing help that you will increase their confidence and instill that sense of belief.

A favorite conversation game of mine as a leader was to play "if I were you." It went something like this. A team member would come to me with an issue or problem or an idea he or she did not know how to go about getting off the ground. I would let the person talk to me about the situation, listening carefully to hear whether this was an issue of a lack of knowledge, a lack of belief, or both. My response either way was to say, "If I were you …" What followed after were words designed to draw out from them some knowledge that they already possessed but weren't perhaps thinking about. For example, if you came to me and said I am bored, if I would reply that, I were you, I would think of something that you enjoy doing and see if it possible to go do that. Ok remedial example I know but hopefully you get the idea. The point though was not for me to give the answers but to let them think it through for themselves. In doing so it gave the employee confidence and installed in them a sense of personal belief.

We can all think back to conversations we have had with our boss. When all we wanted was advice, they gave us a rah-rah speech; when all we wanted was to know that they had our backs, we got a diatribe of information. This is the literal point of playing "if I were you": to put myself in the employees' shoes and understand whether they need tactical help, emotional support, or both. (Remember that I said all leaders need empathy?)

Did I always get the questions right? Of course not. Sometimes I can give great advice, but only sometimes, not always. Even the best advice is wasted on someone who just needs to hear a kind word. I don't think anyone really expects perfection every time. If a flawed person in authority like me, like you, can be wrong, then it is okay for your team to be wrong. Showing you're human as a leader, and thus inherently error-prone, is arguably the best way to show empathy and instill personal belief.

I worked closely with a lady who lacked confidence. She was not a direct report of mine but we sat very close to each other in the workplace and we talked to each other, a lot. Perhaps too much. On paper we did not have a great deal in common. I was an executive and she was an administrative assistant. She spoke carefully and discreetly while I tended to run my mouth. We had vastly differing social and political views. But I truly liked her, respected her, and believed she had a lot to offer. She just lacked some personal belief in her abilities. More importantly she lacked someone to believe in her unconditionally. But I believed in her. As such I asked her to join an informal peer relationship group that I had with other employees.

The peer relationship group were employees who were not direct reports of mine, but ones in whom I felt had a great deal of potential that just needed to be unleashed. Each month we would sit down together and discuss what was going with their career, goals, needs etc.

At first this particular lady did not speak up too much at our discussions. Mostly I would just help her with some information she would need for a task or just be a sympathetic ear for her to vent. Realizing that by just being an informative ear was not really helping her overcome her lack of confidence, I started to play the "if I were you game" with her. At first she doubted that she could think through the answers for herself. She was very hesitant to be a partner in this game. But I knew one of her strengths was that she was a great mother and a loving grandmother. No easy job either of those right? All I needed to do was to tap into that core of her she was. So I would try to make all my "if i were you" replies around her role as a parent. It worked. She began viewing tasks and goals as no longer beyond her capability. Over time she flourished and gained confidence. And I was thrilled to bits.

Before I leave this, I want to give you an "if I were you." If I were you, I'd be very aware that there is, or can appear to be, a fine line between giving advice and telling an employee what to do. In my experience it is better to not play the game than have your team members think you are just telling them what to do. Telling them what to do negates their own ability to critically think about a situation. If playing the game is repeated over time, this will eventually stifle their creativity, lower their confidence, and lead to disengaged employees. All the hard work you have done acting with fairness, taking care of their health, and speaking up on their behalf will count for naught. Your team will become like Scott's, just waiting for the next command. As a result it will be moving slowly and painfully toward a similar emotional, if not physical, fate.

As a leader you have a sphere of influence, and that sphere has an effect on company morale and culture. Sadly, however, many leaders see influencing culture as outside of their job scope, or too hard, or too unconventional to even be given a second thought. Leaders often believe that somehow culture is an inherent part of the company, or worse, something that is dictated by owners and presidents. It is a convention that few are willing to trifle with. It is an obvious truism that culture is heavily influenced by the top, and disproportionately so. By learned behavior most of us just accept this lack of influence and make little or just occasional sporadic attempts to positively change the culture at an organization. Yet contrary to what we might think, we can create a culture for our team, and we can influence the culture of the entire organization. The good news is that it is not hard, but it will require some of that nothing time. Having a leadership contract with your team, whether it is written down or not, is a great place to start.

8. Sextants, Ice Flows, and the Weather

The Antarctic can be a scary, brutal and unpredictable environment. Especially if like Amundsen and Shackleton you undertake courses there that have never been charted before. The business climate can also be equally as unpredictable. Climate changes can render budgets and strategic plans as valuable as the paper they are printed on. But let's be honest here, the climate of the Antarctic does not in any way compare to where you work. Unless you work in the Antarctic of course, which in that case, my apologies.

Like the Antarctic, the business environment has its freakish weather, uncertain conditions and hidden dangers. What can make understanding the business environment challenging for leaders is that there are actually two climates that must be understood and navigated: the external environment *and* the internal environment. Like the weather, even your company can be hot to your plans one day and cold to them the next. The environments are figuratively like an Antarctic ice flow, constantly moving in uncertain and sometimes dangerous directions. As an unconventional leader, you have to be prepared for when a good weather opportunity presents itself and also for when the prevailing winds start blowing against you. In order to do that, you need a team of good navigators. Navigators who understand the climate, know where they are, and know where they want to go.

Before Amundsen, Scott, or Shackleton could even set one foot upon the cold Antarctic ice caps, they had to do many things: raise money, purchase dogs, get a ship, etc. In order to raise money, they had to identify, engage, and excite potential donors of their planned polar exploits. (FYI, in the business world, any audacious goal your team plans will need you to similarly identify, engage, and excite stakeholders.) In order to acquire sledding dogs, they had to find out which breed was most suited to the Antarctic conditions and where to find the canines. Getting a ship was not the walk in the park you might think either. The ship had to be sturdy enough to carry years' worth of supplies (and dogs!) and strong enough to be able to resist being crushed in ice. Anyway, the point to all this is that the explorers had to do a lot of hard work before they could even begin their journey.

In reading this far into the book, you have hopefully started to do your hard work. If you have started implementing some of the suggestions, you are on your way to having a team of skilled and engaged navigators. Trust me, having good navigators, both literally and figuratively, is very important. I'll explain.

I mentioned in a previous chapter the name Frank Worsley. He was Shackleton's navigator (real not hypothetical) on the *Endurance* expedition. Through his achievements, Worsley proved he was undoubtedly an incredible navigator, and as such a great asset to his leader and team. While Shackleton was the big-picture guy who could see a way out of the team's dire situation and lead his team to safety, it was Worsley who could navigate them to safety. There are a number of astonishing feats of navigational ability that Worsley achieved during the *Endurance* team's voyage to safety. Of them all, perhaps the feat of sailing the twenty-foot boat *James Caird* across eight hundred miles of open ocean, searching for the proverbial needle in a haystack that was the safety of South Georgia Island, is arguably the most remarkable. In order to find the island, Worsley had at his disposal a sextant. A what? A sextant. A sextant is a device used to measure the angle between any two objects. Sailors could use a sextant to determine location by using the sun and stars as the objects. This would be challenging enough in calm seas on a steady boat. But on the *James Caird* in rough seas with little visibility, it was truly astonishing that Worsley could navigate the team so close to its desired destination.

Now before you put this book down and rush online to buy sextants and other more modern global positioning systems, this chapter isn't about actual navigating. But there are parallels here that as unconventional leaders we can draw from. While it is without question your duty as a leader to lead, you also need to have a team that knows how to navigate. This is not the type of navigation that will help team members find their next meeting room or the closest Starbucks. It is the type of navigation that will help you demonstrate leadership, help your team have a better understanding of what drives the business, and help you all reach your version of South Georgia Island.

There are many clichés in business and perhaps the most commonly expressed is "There is no *i* in team." (Clichés are bad and mine can be worse.) But here's another cliché that should be used just as commonly: "There is no leadership without a 'ship.'" It goes without saying that if you're going to take a journey, there is a need for a ship (boat, plane, car, etc.). You could walk, but unless the destination is close, it would take forever. The literal difference between a leader and leadership then is a ship. As a result, without a journey or destination, you're just a leader. Ouch, told you. That's bad (please see the later chapter on not being perfect). If you are content to just float along on the same spot, great. You may well be a leader, just without showing any real leadership.

Unconventional leaders don't bop along on the same spot however. They take a team on a journey. Why? Because they know the environments will change, and they don't want to be stuck with their team on an uncertain ice flow. Unconventional leaders as a result have to show leadership. Coaching your team members to become good navigators is an important step in demonstrating real leadership. If you have done your skills analysis, gotten your team motivated and engaged, and established a leadership contract, then you are ready to take the team on a journey. And you have already led it to the starting point, base camp.

WHERE ARE YOU? BASE CAMP.

In all journeys there are at least two definitive points: a beginning and an end. While convention tends to focus on the destination, knowing the starting point is equally as important. Despite that most obvious of navigational truths, I have spent endless hours (and days) in strategy discussions talking at length about where we should be going with, at best, one or two minutes about where the organization is now. The answer is just so obvious that is does not require attention. But the answer is not obvious, and it does require attention. Why? Because so many teams actually have no idea where they really are (figuratively, not literally) and because where you are is your base camp, the starting point of any strategic journey.

As an executive of five functional areas that had multiple levels of management, I received lots of monthly reports. Despite the time it would take, and some advice from my peers that told me they never read monthly reports, I chose to read them all. I utilized some of my nothing time to read the reports because with managers all across the country, let alone all across the world, the monthly report was the most regular and succinct way for my team to tell me what was going on. An environmental update as it were. There's nothing unconventional about a monthly report. It was a staple of where I have worked and probably where you work. What is unconventional though, beyond just reading them, is critically looking beyond the data and graphs to see if your team really does know that most basic rule of navigation: where are we? Shockingly many employees don't.

In reading the reports, I quickly noticed that when there were good months, the managers would write that it was, generally, due to weather, great products, and great service. When the months were not so good, it was due to the weather, competition, or both. Staying true to my "banker" genetics and curious about if this "weather" thing was a conventional trend, I did some research. I asked a waitress at a successful local restaurant if she knew why it was so popular. She told me customers chose to eat at the restaurant because the food was good and reasonably priced and the service was efficient. Good for them. Later that day I went to a well-known retail store that was, to be honest, well, sparse of human life. I asked an employee by the cash register if she knew why the store was so empty. She believed that the lack of traffic was due to the economy, the weather (!), and the negative media that this particular store had been experiencing. While a sample of two is hardly sufficient to form the basis of any corroborative evidence, it did strike me that the successful business saw its success as being driven purely by internal factors, while the unsuccessful business saw its lack of potential customers as being connected to purely external ones. My team in its monthly reports had not even been going into the depth that the waitress or store clerk had done. To the team members, it was always predominantly weather. In the bad months, weather. In the good months, weather. Outside of the weather, they were not communicating that they really did know where they were (figuratively, again). The word "weather" was promptly banned from all future reports.

So why the prohibition on the word "weather"? Because it is just too obvious, too easy, and too lazy. I do not need to have any experience as a theme park manager to know that if it is sunny and mild outside, my park will be busier than when it is cold and blowing a blizzard. The word "weather" (or its industry equivalent) prevents us from actually taking a good, hard look at what really is happening. I know, I know, convention says we must talk about the weather. If you ever have heard a company report its financial results, you will hear weather mentioned, a lot. So weather is not an uncommon crutch. But it isn't a free pass.

Perhaps the challenge for many us is being able to think through and write down an honest, repeat that, honest assessment of the current state of the business—an assessment in terms of the internal environment (quality of the product, service, etc.) and the external environment (lack of customers, economy, etc.). It requires an openness to believe things might not be all that great or that we really do not understand why one month is good and another bad. Or even worse, that we have no understanding of how the internal and external environments impact the day-to-day business.

Thus an important skill required of any unconventional leader is the ability to take a step back and critically help his or her team members make an honest, regular assessment of where they are, why they are there, and what they are going to do about it. There is absolutely no point, none whatsoever, in any company employee focusing on process improvement, cost management, speed to market, or anything else for that matter if the outcomes of those measures are in diametric opposition to the trending needs of the external environment: your customer. If you do, you will be aimlessly floating on your icecap while the external environment moves further and further away from you (figuratively, of course, but also literally).

It is important to understand that while having no ability to control the actual weather, we can and do affect the way our teams perceive the climate. On their respective journeys to the South Pole, both the Amundsen and Scott teams were essentially in the same weather. They traveled in the same place on earth, at the same time, albeit a week or so apart. Amundsen and his team, in their recordings of the trip, reported weather as more of an afterthought, as if the biting cold, blowing snow, and icy conditions were a hurdle they clearly had already understood would exist. Scott's team appeared to have been surprised by the inclement conditions, and Scott's own diary bemoaned their lack of good weather fortune.[8] Whether one agrees or disagrees with Scott, we can certainly appreciate that he may well have been surprised by the conditions. Weather after all can be very unpredictable. His attitude about the conditions though did spread through his team. Apsley Cherry-Garrard, the youngest on Scott's team, who stayed at base camp and did not make the journey to the South Pole, and thus survived, reminisced that the weather had been worse than expected. There were no similar reports from Amundsen's team.[9] His team either saw it differently or knew not to talk about it. I like to think Amundsen would have understood and approved of my weather word ban.

Establishing your base camp is just as critical to you as it was for Amundsen or Scott. It is worth the time and effort beyond a few words to build a good one. Because without knowing where you are, getting to your journey will be so much harder, and quite possibly, a pointless exercise.

WHERE DO YOU WANT TO GO? THE VISION.

A leader of a team without a journey to take or a goal to reach has a team resting on the same spot, heading neither forward or backward. If you are resting, I can almost guarantee that neither the environmental conditions nor your competitors are resting. So just bopping along on the same spot is not an option, even in good weather. If you're going to take a strategic journey and you have your ship (your team), guess who needs to captain that ship? You. Your first task as captain of the strategic journey was figuring out where you are now.

---

[8]   Leonard Huxley, ed.
[9]   Apsley Cherry-Garrard.

Your second role? Figuring out where you want to go and leading your team to get there.

The good news is that developing a vision really is the easy, fun part. The hard and sometimes tedious work of figuring out where you are is behind you. But that doesn't mean it is going to be all smooth sailing. But if there is ever an opportunity to keep your team engaged, excited, and motivated, and utilize all those skills you now know it has, establishing a vision is it. Like many visions the difficult part will be the first hurdle: figuring out where exactly you want to go.

Your primary responsibility as captain is to establish the vision. But, Neill, aren't there tons of books written and courses created to help with establishing and managing a strategic vision? Well, yes, there are. Some of them are actually pretty good too. But if you have ever saved money for something, joined a gym to get fit, worked toward a college degree, or cooked a meal, you already have some strategic vision setting and implementation experience. The process behind getting fit or having friends over for dinner is in essence the same process, if not quite on the same scale.

Think about a vision to lose weight. Your vacation is coming and you want to look good. You have the vision of a sleeker, fitter version of yourself. To achieve that vision you set a goal to tone up your body and lose thirty pounds. You might need to join a gym and actually go to it every now and then. In order to go to the gym you need gym clothes, so you go to the store and buy some. You decide that a good strategic goal is to reduce your caloric intake and eat healthier. So you throw away all the cookies and chips and frozen pizzas and buy vegetables, fruit, and lean meats and start counting calories every day. Not particularly complicated, right? But it all started with your vision of the sleeker, possibly hotter, version of yourself. Before your team can plan anything, it will need a vision from you.

So you want to have a vision but are not sure of what exactly, and you don't really know where to begin. Well, for a start the vision needs to contain certain elements to meet the strategy sniff test. It absolutely must be quantifiable, and your team members need to know if they have achieved it or not. It must be compelling to your team and to your boss. It must be challenging enough to get your team excited and engaged. While it is likely that you will be engaged in becoming healthier and that your employees will be excited to see a sleeker version of you, it is probably not a compelling enough vision to get them too engaged in their job. It also must be realistic. It is hardly realistic for a group of cubicle dwellers with no polar experience to suddenly decide to cross the Antarctic. If only, right? Also your team members are not going to be too excited about using up all their vacation time to take a trip to the South Pole. I bet your boss won't be thrilled with your long absence either. Sniff test fails. But what these rather poor examples do demonstrate is that strategic visions are generally one of three things: a financial number, (lose twenty pounds), an achievement (getting into those new jeans), or a milestone (one hundred days at the gym). All those visions are quantifiable, and you will know if you have achieved it or not.

So what is going to be compelling for your team? Well, as we now know, it has to be related to your team's primary task. It also has to be obtainable. If your team feels like there are too many internal or external environmental factors at play, giving it little control over success, then the vision will not be compelling for the team members. Is the vision over a longer period of time than just a year or so? A longer vision gives your team a sense of comfort by relieving the pressure to achieve success immediately. For example, if your vision is to have one thousand likes on your Facebook page and you are already at 990, it isn't that much of a stretch to believe the vision will be obtained sooner rather than later, and it quite likely is not that much of a challenge. If the vision is to have one million likes, it quite likely isn't too realistic either. The last thing a vision should do is set you and your team up for failure.

So there are really only six questions you need to ask yourself before presenting any vision to your team:

1. Is the vision a financial number, achievement, or milestone?
2. Is the vision quantifiable?
3. Is the vision in line with the primary task of your functional area?
4. Is the vision a short- or long-term goal?
5. Is the vision challenging but also achievable?
6. Is the vision compelling to your team (and your boss)?

But, Neill, what about all those chapters in those strategy books written about this? Surely it is much more complicated than six questions. Nope, it really is that simple. The difficult and challenging part is strategically developing and managing goals and tasks in order to achieve the vision. You know like selecting the right gym and buying the right workout pants. But that is why you now have a great, motivated, engaged team and why you are now a leader that your team is willing to follow. It would be a foolish mistake to believe that you could get your team to the vision starting line without its members first being inspired, motivated, and engaged, and an unbelievable amount of hubris to think that you and they could ever get close to the finish line without maintaining the inspiration, motivation, and engagement.

TOOLS FOR PREVENTING MADNESS

So you are the captain of your ship and you are in charge and you have a vision destination. You know who is to blame when that ship hits a rock, gets incased in solid frozen ice, or just simply goes off course? That's right, your team. You thought I was going to say you right?

Well your team includes you so I actually did. As much as you should share the success you should also share the burden when things go awry. An engaged and motivated team does not want a boss who puts everything on their shoulders. They want a boss that is sane.

Even with the best team and the best vision and the best strategic goals, stuff you were not expecting to happen is going to happen. But at the end of the day, is it still the team's responsibility to take ownership of any accidental slip ups in judgment and strategy miscues. It is equally your responsibility to help your team manage the strategic tasks and learn from any accidental rock hitting. To do that you are going to have to accept an unconventional idea about leadership: all leaders are not perfect.

Despite being a meticulous planner, Amundsen accepted un-equivocally that he was not perfect, that all his planning might not be perfect, and that his team might not be perfect. Right up until the final moments before leaving the Antarctic base camp for the journey to the South Pole, Amundsen was rethinking and refining every step, literally, right down to the men's clothing and boots. Equally so, I am not perfect, your team is not perfect, and you are not perfect. Not being perfect and not knowing everything is not a weakness like convention would have us believe, but rather believing and acting like you are perfect is. Actually it is hubris. As a result we should all constantly evaluate how we are doing as a team, our progress toward the vision, whether or not the strategic goals and tasks are showing up in results, and, perhaps most importantly, if we are all still engaged in the journey. Remember earlier in the book when I talked about process improvements and scorecards? Well, here is where the best process improvements and the real need for scorecards come into play. If you are not measuring employee engagement then you might as well not measure anything.

Real navigation occurs during a journey. As captain you must lead not create, and delegate not pontificate on every task and maneuver.

You really won't be able to anyway, and if you attempt to, you will go crazy. Fortunately there are systems and tools you can implement that will prevent you from going mad. These include, though probably are not limited to:

1. Creating an engaging and meaningful scorecard.
2. Establishing weekly goals on Monday and checking progress throughout the week.
3. Creating monthly SMART goals (X to Y by when). These goals should be specific, measurable, attainable, realistic, and timely (or SMART).
4. Delegating individual goals and assessing progress weekly.
5. Reviewing outcomes. Are the chosen individual goals getting your team closer to the goal?
6. Establishing information conduits for internal and external environment information.
7. Maintaining a balanced dashboard of critical current and predictive metrics.
8. Regularly sharing and discussing goals with stakeholders for critical feedback.
9. Repeat. 'Cause you are still not perfect.

Before we leave navigation, just one more cautionary tale from the explorers: look out for crevasses. A *crevasse* is a deep crack in an ice sheet or glacier. Crevasses form as a result of the stress generated when two semirigid pieces above have different rates of movement. The resulting intensity of the stress causes a breakage. While you and your team should remain committed to the goal and destination, crevasses in the form of unexpected bumps will occur, and you should be flexible enough with your plans to take a detour every now and then. When an unexpected crevasse appeared before Amundsen, Shackleton, and

Scott, they didn't try to go on in the same planned direction. That would have been foolish and quite possibly deadly. Leading your team toward a crevasse would be equally as foolish. Yet many leaders do just that. They become so single-minded on a particular goal, they become blind to what actually is in front of their team. Unless you think a future in a cold bottomless pit sounds like fun, don't go there. And don't lead your team there.

> Superhuman effort isn't worth a damn unless it achieves results.
>
> —ERNEST SHACKLETON

Just a quick note on the previous quote. I agree with Mr. Shackleton on this one, and so do many other leaders. Just remember that you are a people-first leader. As a people-first leader you should define results in more than just sales growth numbers and debt to equity ratios. You should define results in the engagement level of your team. Having an engaged team is the single most important result of all. It is the one result from which all others will either be achieved or not.

9. Honesty

Honesty? Really? Surely you may be saying to yourself, honesty is a convention that cannot be challenged. Well, yes it can. Why? Because what appears as honest behavior at one company would never be tolerated at another. Some bosses want you to be completely open with them about what is going on. Others would rather you keep your opinions to yourself. As a result it can be confusing for leaders to grasp how to do all the things required of them and be still open and honest about it.

Honesty by convention can be subjective. If this were a philosophy book, I could spend the next few days having you read page after page about the arguments on whether it is okay to tell a lie or withhold the truth. But thankfully for you, and me, this book is about leadership. Being dishonest, whether it is withholding information or telling a part truth, is a part of organizational life. It is like guys peeing in the shower. Nobody wants to talk about it, yet they all have done it. If they tell you differently, well, they are just figuratively peeing in the shower.

Leaders do things that nobody wants to hear about and that they don't want to talk about. Accept that it is going to happen. As an unconventional leader though, you should try to mitigate the amount of, well, shower peeing. Fortunately for you this is a short chapter, so I have spared you from having to relive your college philosophy class days. But this is an important issue and deserves at least a little of our time.

Okay, I need you to cut me a little slack here and indulge me for a bit. There are many stories and parables that have been written about honesty. Even though it has absolutely nothing to do with polar exploration or basset hounds, the parable below of the emperor's seeds is one of my favorites. The lesson is universal and seems highly appropriate for the workplace, especially when it comes to talking honestly about a failed task or goal.

The Emperor's Seeds
Author Unknown

Once there was an emperor in the Far East who was growing old and knew it was coming time to choose his successor. Instead of choosing one of his assistants or one of his own children, he decided to do something different.

He called all the young people in the kingdom together one day. He said, "It has come time for me to step down and to choose the next emperor. I have decided to choose one of you." The kids were shocked! But the emperor continued. "I am going to give each one of you a seed today. One seed. It is a very special seed. I want you to go home, plant the seed, water it, and come back here one year from today with what you have grown from this one seed. I will then judge the plants that you bring to me, and the one I choose will be the next emperor of the kingdom!"

There was one boy named Ling who was there that day and he, like the others, received a seed. He went home and excitedly told his mother the whole story. She helped him get a pot and some planting soil, and he planted the seed and watered it carefully. Every day he would water it and watch to see if it had grown.

After about three weeks, some of the other youths began to talk about their seeds and the plants that were beginning to grow. Ling kept going home and checking his seed, but nothing ever grew. Three weeks, four weeks, five weeks went by. Still nothing.

By now the others were all talking about their plants, but Ling didn't have a plant, and he felt like a failure. Six months went by and there was still nothing in Ling's pot. He just knew he had killed his seed. Everyone else had trees and tall plants, but he had nothing. Ling didn't say anything to his friends, however. He just kept waiting for his seed to grow.

A year finally went by and all the youths of the kingdom brought their plants to the emperor for inspection. Ling told his mother that he wasn't going to take an empty pot. But she encouraged him to go, to take his pot, and to be honest about what happened. Ling felt sick to his stomach, but he knew his mother was right. He took his empty pot to the palace.

When Ling arrived, he was amazed at the variety of plants grown by all the other youths. They were beautiful, in all shapes and sizes. Ling put his empty pot on the floor, and many of the other kids laughed at him.

A few felt sorry for him and just said, "Hey, nice try."

When the emperor arrived, he surveyed the room and greeted the young people. Ling just tried to hide in the back. "My, what great plants, trees, and flowers you have grown," said the emperor. "Today one of you will be appointed the next emperor!"

All of a sudden, the emperor spotted Ling at the back of the room with his empty pot. He ordered his guards to bring him to the front.

Ling was terrified. "The emperor knows I'm a failure! Maybe he will have me killed!"

When Ling got to the front, the emperor asked his name. "My name is Ling," he replied. All the kids were laughing and making fun of him. The emperor asked everyone to quiet down. He looked at Ling and announced to the crowd, "Behold your new emperor! His name is Ling!"

Ling couldn't believe it. He couldn't even grow his seed. How could he be the new emperor?

Then the emperor said, "One year ago today, I gave everyone here a seed. I told you to take the seed, plant it, water it, and bring it back to me today. But I gave you all boiled seeds, which would not grow. All of you, except Ling, have brought me trees and plants and flowers. When you found that the seed would not grow, you substituted another seed for the one I gave you. Ling was the only one with the courage and honesty to bring me a pot with my seed in it. Therefore, he is the one who will be the new emperor!"

So what did you think? Some of you may be reflecting after reading "The Emperor's Seeds" that I am somehow encouraging you to devise a similar scheme with your team. The answer is absolutely not. First, your team members are not children. Second, you should never set up anyone on your team to fail, whatever the good intentions behind the set up are. Finally, it is a parable about honestly, and that includes you. What to me as a leader is the most interesting about this parable is that of all the children, only one was honest, while the majority were prepared to lie and cheat in order to be successful. It says something about the culture that the majority would be okay with actions that were clearly dishonest as long as the outcome seemingly satisfied the emperor. It is sadly a culture we also see in the workplace. (As an aside, it also says something of the unconventional nature of an emperor who would put aside commonly accepted traditions of heredity and not have one of his own children be the chosen new emperor).

It is so easy in the workplace to fall into the trap of telling leaders what they want to hear or doing what you think your boss wants you to do. But you will just be telling your boss what *you* think he or she wants to hear, and you will just be doing what *you* think he or she wants you to do. In the example of "The Emperor's Seeds," the children and parents did what they thought the emperor wanted them to do, and they acted dishonestly in order to do it. They were wrong. Unless you have direct-line access to the thoughts and motivations of your boss, there is a good chance you may be wrong too. You will also be contributing to a culture that values achievement over ethics and honesty. And you will be sending a dangerous message to your team. As a result the team members could end up being dishonest to you about what they are doing and are capable of doing.

There will be times when you develop a vision, a budget, or a goal that really is almost impossible. Yes, that convention, that you can do anything. (Remember Kelly Clarkson's quarterback days)? Untrue, mostly. Take for example the exploits of Shackleton and his team. No team until 2013 has even attempted to follow in Shackleton's footsteps and re-create the eight-hundred-nautical-mile journey from Elephant Island to South Georgia in the *James Caird*. There is a reason why not. That is because it was an astounding, once-in-a-lifetime type of achievement, and many, most, or all teams would fail at replicating it. You and your team have to be honest with each other and all stakeholders about what is and what is not accomplishable. I am all for a BHAG (big, hairy, audacious goal) but not to the risk of sacrificing a culture that values honesty. You also have to be honest with each other about what you can achieve on a short-term basis. Don't over promise or under deliver. It is as good as being dishonest.

10. *Unconventional*

You got this far, so I guess you are now waiting for me to tell you just how to go about being unconventional. Well I have given you the platform. It is now up to you to build the rest. If I told you exactly how to be unconventional, I would in practice be going against the very important lesson I want you to learn; being unconventional means doing things that you believe are right for you, right for your team, and right for your business. All I have done is to give you examples of how I was unconventional and discussed what conventions may be holding you back. I have also hopefully given you the confidence to be unconventional.

Will people understand your sudden urge to go rogue? Probably not. Will people notice you doing things differently? More than likely. Will you feel different about the way you lead and the ways you demonstrate leadership? Absolutely.

By definition, being unconventional means you are going to defy convention. Guess what? People don't usually like having conventional wisdom challenged, especially your boss, or worse, his boss, or even worse than that, your peers. If you are like me, this means you will start questioning (and possibly stop going to) that pointless two-hour Wednesday meeting where nothing of substance is discussed, no meaningful decision is ever made, and you spend most of your time being told to be quiet. It means you will start to question internally accepted practices like the irrelevant questions on your (and your team's) performance review form and propose putting in new ones. It means you will have to go to bat for fairness and equality of pay for your team and in the process have to make a few deals with the devil, sticking your head right onto the chopping block each time. If you are not prepared to put your neck on the line for your team, you cannot expect employees to put theirs on the line for you. Quid pro quo. It means you are going to have to place what at first could be an uncomfortable amount of trust in your team. It means you are going to make some tough decisions, often quickly, and sometimes wrong, which in turn will challenge that trust-in-your-team thing again. It means doing things your natural way and not the way convention tells you to.

How much from this book you actually apply to your leadership life is up to you. Even with the power of Google search and www. writerswholiketostalktotheirreaders.com, I won't be able to track you down and make you do things the unconventional way. But there are four popular conventions around, especially in the business world, that I would implore you to break. They are the conventions of pretending to be someone you're not, looking busy, needing credibility, and expecting loyalty.

Being unconventional is not just doing things differently. It is also about acting differently. What do I mean by different? I mean acting like yourself and not how people expect you to act (your company's policy manual and code of conduct notwithstanding). When I first became an executive, like most senior members of staff I was given an office. It even had a view of the parking lot! At first I never questioned why I needed an office. My boss told me I did and convention says bosses should be in offices. Over time though I started to question whether or not being in an office was really me (remember, first chapter, knowing you). Here is why I questioned it.

Another passion of mine is sports. It is a ridiculous passion given that I will watch just about any sport and I have three times in my life taken vacations just to watch the Olympics on television (thank goodness the term "stay-cation" now has legitimacy). What I would observe in sports, especially team sports, is where the coach or manager would be. Was he in an office? Nope, he was right on the sidelines with his team. Any basketball fan has seen the coach running up and down the sidelines during a game. In soccer, Caleb Porter, coach of the MLS Portland Timbers, rarely sits down during a game. If you watch him during the match you can see him literally observing every move and thinking about every next one. I wanted to be the coach running up and down the sidelines, not the isolated manager sitting in an office. I moved out of the office and into a cubicle, with my team, and turned my old office into an informal meeting space, complete with coffee machine and a sofa. It wasn't a conventional move. Many didn't understand it. But I did, and more importantly, my team did. Am I telling you to move out of your office? No. Absolutely not. What I am telling you is that if being in an office doesn't work for you, doesn't feel right for you, or is simply just not needed for your job, then don't be in one. In the unconventional leadership world as in life, actions speak louder than words.

Another convention I happily broke was the "your desk must be full of paper to demonstrate you're busy" rule. Well, that convention is about as garbage worthy as most of that paper on your desk is. But here's a recap of it, as if you need it. Lots of papers and files and Post-its and stuff on your desk sends the signal that you're busy, overworked, and preferably not to be disturbed, 'cause you're so busy. Convention demands that we be busy, or at a minimum look busy, so I get it, kind of. But just remember as a leader it also sends this same message: I'm busy, too busy to talk to you and be of any help to you. That cannot be good for team morale, can it? I am not sure if my team members ever knew if I was busy or not, but I never had more than the occasional

Post-it stuck to my computer or the odd paper sitting on top of my desk. I would like to think that they knew I was available to them (usually the same reason why I skipped those Wednesday afternoon meetings). So should you quickly put this book down and clean up your workspace? Of course you should if it's full of "look busy pieces of paper." Seriously, do it. And while you're at your desk, schedule those free blocks of time on your work calendar to do nothing. That's right, nothing.

I scheduled a lot of nothing time. Indeed, when meetings were scheduled over my nothing time, I would get really annoyed by the accepted truism that a meeting, any meeting, must be way more important than my doing-nothing time. During my nothing time, I would do the unthinkable; get up out of my chair, walk somewhere, and talk to somebody, in person. Remember face-to-face talking, like we did before e-mail? One day while walking back down a hallway, returning to my desk with a donut (okay, and a cookie), an employee remarked how I must have a sixth-sense-like ability to be able to sniff out free food around the company. You know my secret to being able to sniff out free food? I walked around the company, sometimes because I wanted to have a needed conversation with somebody in person, and sometimes just to say hi and chat with other employees.

I can just imagine what the naysayers are thinking right now. It goes along the lines of "Well, Neill, I am way too busy to schedule nothing time, and you must not have been very busy to begin with, given that you didn't have any paper on your desk." Imagined point taken. Time, though, is like that other thing you wished you had more of; money. If you spend it all, you won't have anything saved for emergencies, or vacations, or that sweater that you absolutely must have but will still end up in the Goodwill bin six months from now. In order to do the things that give you pleasure but cost money, you need to save money. Scheduling nothing time is just the hours and minutes version of dollars and cents. In order to be an effective leader, you need to have time saved for coaching, mentoring, and just generally being with your team. If you are hungry, you also need to save time as there is probably a lot of free food around your workplace right now.

Still not convinced and a donut not enough of an inducement? Then think back to the last time at work you experienced a crisis that required your immediate attention. Remember how it took you away from those papers and Post-its on your desk? It was a crisis so most likely you had to deal with it straight away. In response to the crisis, you also probably had to delegate whatever you were working on. Was the crisis managed and resolved? Yes, probably. But guess what else you did? You found the trick to scheduling nothing time through delegation. You also, in delegating a task, showed trust in one of your team. And amazingly, you survived a workday without your precious paper and Post-its.

The convention of credibility might be a mystery to many of you, but it is real and very much present in the workplace. Credibility is defined by Merriam-Webster's dictionary as "the quality of being believed or accepted as true, real, or honest."[10] Other sources describe credibility as having both objective and subjective components. Yet the reality is that the parts that make up a person's believability, honesty, and realness are far more objective than subjective. If you do not believe me, talk to any person who has ever undergone a 360-Leadership evaluation by his or her peers and colleagues. I can (almost) guarantee you that no person is perceived in the same way by every person he or she works with.

In the business world, we accept credibility as meaning that a person has the technical ability to do a job and has the required prerequisites (degree, experience, etc.). Yes, we fall back on that technical skill and experience standard I mentioned at the start of the book. A perusal on many job postings will glean lines like "must have five

---

[10] http://www.merriam-webster.com/dictionary/credibility.

years experience in this" or " have knowledge of this software system". The experience and knowledge is what give us credibility. While that is quite probably true, it seems to ignore factors that can make a candidate a good employee; their emotional intelligence. The fact that a potential employee has a high degree of trust, or has proven to be honest, or has demonstrated a consistent work behavior seems to go out the door when evaluating their credibility. This conventional norm seems particularly true when it comes to hiring new positions and promoting existing employees. It is to the latter of those two that perhaps my biggest leadership regret occurred.

In 2008 I had the honor of hiring the world's best employee. This is not hyperbole. Okay, maybe a little, but to me, she was the level-headed, strategic-focused, process-orientated, people-minded foil to my slightly more scatterbrained "throw out ideas and try them until something works" approach. In a Hollywood movie, she would be the smart one while I would play the irreverent sidekick. Like me, she thought through problems and issues, but probably more calmly and less emotionally than me. She liked to express her opinions openly and honestly, liked data and information (yes, like me), but she intuitively seemed to know the appropriate time to express her opinions and when enough data was enough. Because in her strengths I could see my own weaknesses so clearly, she inspired me to want to be a better employee and leader.

Three years into our partnership I was promoted to a new role, leaving my existing role vacant. The decision on who to hire to replace me should have been a no-brainer. She was the obvious candidate to me as the basic elements of my perception of credibility were all there. The only piece missing was the experience. The employee did not have any experience managing sales channels at the management level, let alone at the executive level. Knowing she would have to pass the sniff test of not only my boss and the human resources department, but also my boss's boss and his boss, I knew that hiring her into the role would be a huge act of defying convention and would almost certainly not be allowed to proceed by one or all of my required approvers. After a few conversations with some of them, I bought into the required credibility convention. All ideas of putting her into my old position went away. I genuinely convinced myself that this was the right decision for her, the right decision for the team, and the right decision for the company. I sat down with her and explained why she needed sales management experience, at least at some level, and she agreed. Secretly though, between you and me, I don't think she ever fully agreed. Remember, she was smarter than me. She was right of course. I trusted her and her ability; she was honest and always genuine. There could not have been a better candidate.

To understand what makes buying into this convention, of all conventions, my biggest regret, you only have to go back to where we started in the second paragraph of the second chapter. Back at the beginning, if you remember, I had been given almost the exact same opportunity. That unconventional leader had put his head on the line for me. I should have done the same. In subjecting myself to the convention of credibility, I made what I believe was my worst professional error of judgment during my time as a leader, proving that not only am I not perfect but that even the most unconventional mind-set can fall victim to rules of convention.

By going against conventional notions of credibility you will open your mind to giving opportunities to your team. Those opportunities don't just include promotions. They also include giving them new goals, increased responsibilities, and more challenging tasks. For you to clear your time and your desk, you will have to delegate. If your mind is too conditioned to not intuitively trust your team to take on new goals, share in the responsibilities, and take on some of your burned, then you may find yourself quickly falling back to being over worked and over stressed. You will start failing to schedule nothing time and in the process start failing your team as a leader.

Which leads us to loyalty. Please don't demand or expect loyalty. Ever see those commercials on television where the product pitch centers on how you deserve something? You know, you deserve that new car, or that vacation in Hawaii, or to lose those extra pounds. Well, you don't have to deserve it, you just have to work for it. Instead of demanding loyalty as if it was some job-given right or a seven-day trip to Maui, earn it, you know, the old-fashioned way, with hard work. In my experience, loyalty comes too easy to people with some executive adjective at the head of their title. Their relationships with their employees are built on an unyielding acceptance that loyalty is first and foremost. Well, if the failure of the Scott expedition has taught us anything, it should be that you're heading down a dangerous pathway if you expect loyalty, both for you and for your team's morale. With your banked nothing time, you have plenty of hours and minutes to work on building loyalty and not demanding it.

Your banked nothing time should also allow you plenty of time to work on finding yourself, building and getting to know your team members, inspiring them, setting goals with them, and changing the culture with them. Most importantly you should also be having fun with them.

I said in the introduction that this book would be a journey. To go on the journey to being an unconventional leader there has to be a starting point. That starting point is you. If you remember back to Psychology 101 class you will probably remember Socrates saying an unexamined life was not worth living. Not examining who we are leads us to accept things as they are. Our work life is no exception. We look to others to know what it takes to be successful. We imitate the leaders around us, flattering them, whether they motivate or inspire us or not. But the person we should be turning to is ourself. Imitation, at least in this book, is not the sincerest form of flattery. Imitation merely leads us to model behaviors that may or may not help us. It ends up sapping away our creative and innovative needs. It crushes our individuality. It leads us to conform and to accept convention. We end up, as Socrates would probably also have told us, with a work life not worth living. Not examining who you are, what your needs are, what motivates and inspires you, leaves you just modeling your career after somebody else's life. And who knows, that persons life might actually be quite boring. Who wants to be boring?

As part of getting to know yourself, also know that you will soon need to start learning to let go of fear. Yes, fear. You will start to fear that you will be out of step with the rest of your peers. You will fear that there will be consequences for your unconventional actions. You will fear that your new actions are misunderstood and that people will doubt your true intentions. You will start to fear that you cannot change into the type of leader you want to be. These fears are all natural and ones I have experienced many times. Change is, after all, a journey.

It takes courage and strength of character to rebel against convention and start a revolution, but that is exactly what I hope you do. By now I hope you understand that I do not mean a revolution in the "go out and arm yourself with weapons and overthrow you boss" sense. But I do want you to arm yourself with information that leads to a confidence that will allow you to be your true self as a leader. In turn this can lead to a fundamental change in how leadership is viewed across all workplaces.

As well as a revolt, a revolution can also be described as a circular motion. It is in the act of revolting against convention and in the motion of your constant personal evolution that you will find yourself on a journey toward developing into a happier and more engaged employee and leader.

Now I ask you, before reading the last few pages of this book, to do one thing for me. Visualize if you can how it would feel and look like for you to work in an environment that embraces your unique identity and talents. To be a part of a group that is highly engaged and energized to achieve goals and targets. Where your boss is available to provide help and support, not just assign tasks and yell. To be associated with an organization that does not just pride itself on a people-first approach, but actually lives the ethos. If this is the type of place you visualize then isn't the conventional pathway a road worth getting away from? Isn't becoming an unconventional leader a personal revolution worth starting? I believe it is. I hope you do too.

11. The End?

I am sure you have gotten to the end of this book in a reasonable time period. That is intentional, not laziness on my behalf. Seriously. Not laziness. This book was written with reasonably short and hopefully informative chapters so you can easily go back and reread it without having to schedule a day off or take a long trip to undergo a refresher. So is this the end? Oh no, far from it. This is not even the beginning. It is just like any good revolution, a change. If you have decided that you want to be unconventional and be part of a revolution in leadership, the real work starts now. To help you I have included below a suggested revolution plan, which is basically this book without most of the words. You will notice there are no real time frames, no punch lists and no "action completed" boxes.

There are no time frames because everybody is different and every leader is going to be different. Some leaders will want to adopt a new thinking style right away; others will need to mull it over. You should, and must, go at the pace with which you are comfortable. Of course that's assuming you even want to do anything. Promise me though that even if you do nothing else, you will take the self personality test and commit to rereading the book with a better understanding of who you are.

There are no punch lists because, well, that is just too conventional for me. Punch lists are for projects or processes. You are not a machine, and you are not a product. You're a living person with feelings, fears and faults.

Finally, there are no action-completed boxes because outside of completing perhaps the self-assessment, none of these actions really will be completed. You will be continually getting to know yourself and your team, your goals will be changing, your task-tracking methods will be becoming more sophisticated, and your desk will need to be kept clean of clutter. And who wants the fun to be over? It should just be starting. Remember, this is just a suggested action plan. You may start working through the steps and develop different, better, or even more unconventional ways and ideas. Share them with me. I would love to hear them. You can reach me at www.neillwallace.com.

I am not perfect, nor is this suggested change plan perfect.
Any book that tells you its program is guaranteed to lead
to success or promises you perfection is being disingenuous
to your ability, potential, and individuality as a leader.
It also sells short the value of making mistakes.

Revolution Plan

- Start scheduling "nothing" time (in case you did not already do this). You are going to need this time. Trust me.
- Take a personality trait assessment. The one that I found worked the best for me was the Core Values Index by Taylor Protocols. However, I am sure there are many others that would work just as well. The key is to find one that works for you. Ask around for suggestions and talk with your boss. Let him or her know why you want to take one.
- Start letting go of fear.
- Conduct a personal skills assessment. Again there are tests available from many companies. I suggest that you do an honest evaluation of yourself first before taking any test. Talk with your boss about what skills are needed for the position and what he or she believes you excel in and what areas you need more coaching with.
- Take some time to think about who inspires you and why they inspire you. If it is a loved one or friend who is around, talk to him or her. If it is a historical figure, learn more about the person.
- Let go of fear (eat a Twix).
- Determine what skills you believe are needed for your team in both the short and long term. Share with your team what you think, and ask for members' input. They may have a

different and, dare I say it, better idea than you about the required skills.

- Determine whether any changes need to be made to individual duties, roles, your area's organizational structure, job titles, etc. Once you know what you would like to do, discuss with your manager and a representative from your organization's human resources department.

- Schedule a meeting to talk with your entire team about culture. Explain clearly why the meeting is being scheduled and give team members some time to prepare. Ask them to be prepared to talk about topics like:
  - What inspires them?
  - The type of work culture they want.
  - What do they like and dislike about the company/department?
  - What is a fun fact about them that the rest of the team may not know?

- If they do not know already, share with them the current short-term plans of the department. End by scheduling a follow-up meeting to discuss any action items (or promises made). At that meeting you will also be doing the next step. Let your team know in advance.

- Create your vision. It does not have to be perfect as your team can help to hone it. But have something for your team to work with.

- As a group, discuss what long-term plans they would like to establish in order to achieve the vision, how they would manage the goals, etc.

- If you are not great or not comfortable with strategic management, there is a good chance that somebody on your team will be. Let that person help you lead the management of the strategic direction (goal tracking, scorecards, etc) you decide to take and empower him or her with authority. It is trust well invested. At the meeting, let your team do most of the talking, but remember, you are the leader so be prepared to step in when needed.

- Let go of fear.
- Establish an environmental work group to examine the internal and external issues that currently and could potentially impact your short- and long-term strategic plans.
- Read your team's monthly reports critically and ask questions.
- Be honest, bold, and direct. Inspire and have fun. Reward your team when you succeed. Discuss failures openly.
- Be free of fear.

Victory awaits him who has everything in order; luck, people call it. Defeat is certain for him who has neglected to take the necessary precautions in time; this is called bad luck.

—ROALD AMUNDSEN

Referenced works

Barczewski, Stephanie. *Antarctic Destinies: Scott, Shackleton, and the Changing Face of Heroism*. London: Hambledon Continuum, 2007.

Cherry-Garrard, Apsley. *The Worst Journey in the World: Antarctic 1910–13*. New York: Barnes and Noble Publishing Inc,, 2004.

Crane, David. *Scott of the Antarctic: A Life of Courage and Tragedy in the Extreme South*. London: HarperCollins, 2005.

Fiennes, Ranulph. *Captain Scott*. London: Hodder & Stoughton, 2003.

Huntford, Roland. *Shackleton*. London: Hodder & Stoughton, 1985.

Huntford, Roland. *The Last Place on Earth*. Modern Library Exploration, 1999.

Huxley, Leonard, ed. *Scott's Last Expedition, Volume I: Being the Journals of Captain R. F. Scott, RN, CVO*. London: Smith, Elder & Co., 1913.

Lansing, Alfred. *Endurance: Shackleton's Incredible Voyage*. 2nd ed. New York: Carroll & Graf, 1999.

Mills, Leif. *Frank Wild*. Whitby, England: Caedmon of Whitby, 1999.

About Me

I was born in Tasmania, Australia, the youngest of four children to immigrant parents from the United Kingdom. While both my parents were nurses, I had no interest growing up in following in their footsteps. Following my parents' divorce, my mother moved us to the United Kingdom, where I learned to perfect what I think is a pretty spot-on English accent. While in the UK, I attended a performing arts school for five years, eventually leaving to focus on my further education. Following a brief return to Tasmania in 1989, I moved to mainland Australia, and then to the United States in 1996. I have lived in Portland, Oregon, since 1999. I became a permanent resident in 2010 and hope to become a citizen in 2017.

I am a sports fanatic and follow passionately Michigan (college football), Queen Park Rangers (English soccer), and North Melbourne (Australian rules football). I like to kayak and I'm a pretty terrible snowboarder, but that doesn't stop me. I love to read historical nonfiction, with polar explorers and the English monarchy my favorite topics. I have been to about forty countries, with South Africa being the most fascinating. London is the city I would love the most to get lost in. Maui has my favorite beaches and the San Juan Islands calms me. I have an nine-year-old rescue dog named Henry, who as I sit here and type this, is snoring loudly on my leg. I wouldn't have it any other way. My friends are the best support system one could ever hope for.

www.neillwallace.com